THE ROAD TO
MISSIONAL

Embracing the Missional Life

THE ROAD TO
MISSIONAL

JOURNEY TO THE
CENTER OF THE CHURCH

MICHAEL FROST

BakerBooks

a division of Baker Publishing Group
Grand Rapids, Michigan

Published by Baker Books
a division of Baker Publishing Group
P.O. Box 6287, Grand Rapids, MI 49516-6287
www.bakerbooks.com

Printed in the United States of America

Library of Congress Cataloging-in-Publication Data
Frost, Michael, 1961–
   The road to missional : journey to the center of the church / Michael Frost.
      p.   cm. — (Shapevine)
   Includes bibliographical references and index.
   ISBN 978-0-8010-1407-9 (pbk. : alk. paper)
   1. Mission of the church. I. Title.
BV601.8.F762 2011
262′.7—dc23   2011023505

The internet addresses, email addresses, and phone numbers in this book are accurate at the time of publication. They are provided as a resource. Baker Publishing Group does not endorse them or vouch for their content or permanence.

11   12   13   14   15   16   17   7   6   5   4   3   2   1

In keeping with biblical principles of creation stewardship, Baker Publishing Group advocates the responsible use of our natural resources. As a member of the Green Press Initiative, our company uses recycled paper when possible. The text paper of this book is composed in part of post-consumer waste.

To Alan Hirsch,
with much love and gratitude
for all our years of creative partnership.

CONTENTS

About the
SHAPEVINE MISSIONAL SERIES

The key purpose of Shapevine the organization is to bring the various elements of missional Christianity—namely, church planting movements, urban mission, the emerging church, the missional church movement, the organic/simple church, and marketplace ministries—into meaningful dialogue around the truly big ideas of our time. Consistent with this purpose, the Shapevine Missional Series in partnership with Baker Books seeks to bring innovative thinking to the missional issues of church planting, mission, evangelism, social justice, and anything in between.

We seek to publish both established authors as well as others who have significant things to contribute but have operated largely under the radar.

The series will focus on three distinctive areas:

- **Living—Practical Missional Orthopraxy**

  Orthopraxy is what makes orthodoxy worth having. We yearn for the experience and continual flow of living out the gospel message in our day-to-day lives for the sake of others. The stories and ideas in the Shapevine Missional Series are aimed at providing practical handles and means to wrap our readers' minds around the idea of living as the people of God, sent into the world with the Spirit and impulse of Jesus himself.

- **Learning—Solid Missional Orthodoxy**

  Jesus both lived and proclaimed a theology of a missional God. His was and is a message of mercy, justice, and goodness toward others. It was this message that erupted into the greatest movement in the history of humankind. The same God who sent his only Son now sends those who follow his Son, in the same manner and with the same message. This is at the heart of a missional theology.

- **Leading—Tools for Missional Leadership**

  Our aim is for the books in this series to serve as tools for pastors, organizational leaders, and church members throughout the world to equip themselves and others as they travel the path of faithfulness in the missional life.

As a global interactive forum, Shapevine allows anyone to both learn and contribute at whatever level suits. To learn more, go to www.shapevine.com or contact us at info@shapevine.com.

Alan Hirsch and Lance Ford

Series Editor's
PREFACE

I have no hard research to back up what I am about to say, but I am willing to stand by it anyway: I think that if we have not already passed the tipping point in relation to the adoption of the idea of missional church, then we are awfully close. From what we know about the sociology of knowledge and the diffusion of innovations, all that it takes for an idea to be *inevitable* in a given population (in this case, the evangelical church in the West) is the adoption by the innovators (2.5 percent) and the early adopters (13.5 percent). In other words, 16 percent is the tipping point in any given population!

From what I can observe, the majority of the best thinkers and our most progressive practitioners have conceded that the missional conversation has both deepened our theology and given our ecclesiology its much-needed basis from which to understand ourselves and negotiate the challenges of the twenty-first century. I, for one, am hopeful because I believe that behind this term is a cluster of ideas, paradigms, and methodologies that contains nothing less than the seeds of hope for the future of Western Christianity. If this is true, then there is a real chance we will see renewal of Western Christianity in our time.

So, the term *missional* is now being appropriated at a massive rate. But so very often this is being done without the foggiest idea of what it actually means and the impact that it should have on our thinking and practices. The simple adoption of vocabulary without grappling with the inner meaning of words always devolves to jargon. I have heard of *missional* Sunday school, *missional* Greek classes, *missional* this, and *missional* that. The danger of this is clear: when everything becomes missional, then nothing becomes missional. This book speaks directly into that situation.

Michael has been one of the finest evangelists in Australia's recent history. In my opinion, he is also one of the world's best mass communicators, bringing biblical depth to large audiences with an almost uncanny cultural verve. At the same time he has also managed to be a leading activist and practitioner of the missional cause, both locally and internationally. But with *this* book he has come of age as a missiologist and a theologian in his own right. And here, I think, we really get to the heart of the purpose of *The Road to Missional*, because it is one of the theologian's essential roles to help us both understand the meaning of the words that shape the people of God, and to guard against the dilution of the world-changing power of those words.

One of the things I love about this book is the fact that Mike's very distinct personality and commitments are evident throughout. Those who know and love this remarkable man (as I do) know that he can be an amazingly winsome, witty conversationalist. But we also know that Mike does not suffer fools lightly and doesn't mince his words either, and so being around him might not always feel comfortable. This is because Mike is a potent mixture of prophet and evangelist—a person who tells truth in two different ways. As evangelist he has been an excellent spokesman for, and recruiter to, Jesus and his cause. As prophet he is as likely to simply kick your butt . . . a role I think he seems to relish at times.

In *The Shaping of Things to Come* and *Exiles*, for instance, he is operating as primarily an evangelist for the cause and only secondarily as prophet. In *The Road to Missional* he is almost exclusively operating in his role as a prophet. And this, dear reader, is going to make you squirm . . . just a little. That is because prophets are demanding, they move our cheese, raise the bar, rail against unfaithfulness, condemn complacency, and disallow the kind of cheap self-congratulation that we are wont to give ourselves and each other. Filled with a sense of holy discontent, they can't abide any efforts to domesticate the message and bring it down to manageable size. In a word, they are purists and we need them now as much as we ever did! To be more specific, this book is needed right at this time—at the very tipping point itself—because it is at this point that we need to be sure we really are on the right track.

In spite of the geographic distances, Mike is my best friend. I have been profoundly enriched by a long personal friendship, indeed a comradeship, that has involved pioneering an international network called Forge, as well as writing three hefty books together . . . and likely more to come. And so here it is my great privilege to write the foreword for this very timely book, the message of which I too must take heed. I recommend you do the same.

Alan Hirsch, Shapevine series editor,
author of *The Forgotten Ways*,
coauthor of *On the Verge* and *Right Here, Right Now*

INTRODUCTION

Using the M-Word

Ten years ago, the term "emerging missional church" would have been unknown. Today it is impossible to go very far—certainly in the church culture of the USA, UK, and Australasia—without encountering the word and the reality it describes.

—John Drane

Of all the sins of which I'm guilty, the promulgation of a buzzword is perhaps the most surprising and insidious. About a decade ago, when I first began writing about what I then referred to as the "emerging missional church," it never occurred to me what would happen when its emergence was complete and the missional church was a widely accepted phenomenon. Well, that time is upon us. The emerging missional church has well and truly emerged. And after all the initial suspicion by church leaders and all the nit-picking debates, the church as a whole now seems quite relaxed about adopting missional categories and using the associated language to describe all kinds of ministries.

We now have missional conferences, missional church planting schemes, and all manner of missional programs. This is not to mention the fact that books on the missional paradigm are becoming a dime a dozen. So much so, in fact, that one author recently suggested to me that the term *missional* is a bit old hat these days and that the shelves are sagging under the burden of missional church literature. Better, he advised, to use a different, more appealing title to engage potential readers. Ten years ago it never would have occurred to me that being missional would become hip, let alone that it could become passé.

If the missional conversation is over, it occurs to me that it probably hasn't really ever been had. That's because "missional" is not a style or a fad. It's not an add-on, the latest church accessory, the newest cool idea for church leaders. The fact that some are suggesting the conversation is over leads me to think that they weren't listening in the first place. My call—and the call of many other missional thinkers and practitioners—was not for a new approach to *doing* church or a new technique for church growth. I thought I was calling the church to revolution, to a whole new way of thinking about and seeing and being the followers of Jesus today. I now find myself in a place where I fear those robust and excited calls for a radical transformation of our ecclesiology have fallen on deaf ears.

When we inoculate our children against life-threatening disease, we do so by allowing a medical practitioner to inject a small amount of that disease into their system to give their little bodies the chance to fight off small, beatable levels of what would otherwise be an insuperable infection. I fear I might have contributed to the inoculation of the church against the truly unconquerable, transformative idea of missional ecclesiology. Perhaps I have made the missional "disease" too manageable for those who, though they like the idea, aren't willing to stop fighting the full infection.

Perhaps we should call a moratorium on the use of the M-word until we have stepped back, taken a deep breath, and reconsidered what we really mean by it.

When I use the M-word, I'm doing so to describe the wholesale and thorough reorientation of the church around mission. Coffee at Starbucks or couches in the church building might be in some measure an indication of this reorientation, but they aren't in themselves the sum total of the call I have been making.

Of course, I'm not the only person calling for this complete paradigm shift for the church. My dear friend and occasional coauthor, Alan Hirsch, has been at the forefront of this movement. Indeed, it was with Alan that I wrote the following challenge in our first book together in 2003:

> In writing this book we are advocating a wholesale change in the way Christians *do* and *be* the church and because of this ours is not necessarily a popular message. We've become disturbingly aware through personal experience and observation that those who advocate such a thoroughgoing recalibration of the church will not always be met with open arms by the prevailing church leadership. And yet we feel compelled to lovingly challenge the church with the task of dismantling so many of the arcane institutional structures it is now beholden to and to bravely face the future with imagination and courage.[1]

Who would have guessed we'd both end up being so popular! But it wasn't just Alan and me. Equally radical were the British authors like John Drane, Martin Robinson, and Stuart Murray, and Americans such as the original missional voices of Darrell Guder, George Hunsberger, Craig Van Gelder, Alan Roxburgh and Lois Barrett. They in turn have been joined by more recent practitioners like Neil Cole, Ed Stetzer, Dan Kimball, Mike Breen, Hugh Halter, Matt Smay, and a host of others. My primary concern is that a new crop of less daring, less radical voices has emerged recently. These not-quite-missional writers and pastors remain resolutely committed to the existing paradigm while recommending we add a certain missional, shall we say, *flavor* to the mix. For them, being missional is more a state of mind than it is a whole new paradigm. They seem to be suggesting we can flavor all our existing programs to be missional without having to renegotiate anything central or core to the current paradigm.

One notable example was an article that appeared recently in a national denominational paper, pointing out to its apparently confused readership what this newfangled word *missional* actually meant. The author of the article explained that missional is a recently coined word (which is true), but it is just an updated nomenclature of the old, well-known, and oft-practiced word *missionary*. And, he continued, since our network of churches has always been a missionary denomination, we don't need to worry ourselves at all about what it means to be missional. Translation: remain calm and carry on. It read like the despotic earl of a small French village in the 1790s explaining to his serfs that any rumors of revolution weren't to be taken seriously. After all, *liberté, fraternité, et egalité* is just another way of saying everything is fine the way it is.

But too many of us have come to the conviction that it is not fine the way it is. We can't just sprinkle a few missional phrases throughout our vision statements and think that, like magic, it will be so. In the West, researchers like George Hunter have concluded that the US is now the largest mission field in the Western Hemisphere, and the fifth largest mission field on earth.[2]

Indeed, emerging generations continue to turn their backs on the church, rejecting it as an institution without necessarily rejecting the faith it should represent. A recent survey of Americans between the ages of 18 and 29 found that 18 percent of them say they attend worship nearly every week or more often. Compare that to the fact that 40 percent say religion is very important in their lives, 41 percent report praying daily, and 53 percent say they are certain of the existence of God.[3] In other words, religious faith is way more popular than church attendance. In fact, church attendance has dropped right across all age groups, with the exception of the baby boomers. Further research recently found that "more [younger unchurched people] would prefer to read an inspirational book than seek inspirational help from a church."[4] It appears church is one of the last places they would go to satisfy their existential or spiritual cravings. This led the researchers to conclude, "Remarkably, only one in six would go to church if seeking spiritual guidance."[5] I'm not sure why they thought that was remarkable. For many of us it is as clear as the nose on our faces. It is the world in which we live, and I don't see any indications this trend will abate. In the same research, more than 80 percent of the unchurched young people surveyed agreed with the statement "Christianity today is more about organized religion than about loving God and loving people."[6] Quite simply, as Leadership Network's Reggie McNeal says, "Disinterest in institutional cultural Christianity will accelerate."[7]

But while all this research casts the future of the church in a poor light, the number of US megachurches (those with more than 2,000 weekly attendees) has leaped to more than 1,300 today—from just 50 in 1970. As *Forbes* pointedly explained:

> Featuring huge stages, rock bands, jumbotron screens, buckets of tears and oodles of money, as well as the enormity of the facilities, pastor personalities and income—over $8.5 billion a year all told—these churches are impressive forces flourishing at staggering rates.[8]

But at what cost? If there are more megachurches today and less church attendees than ever, it doesn't take a genius to work out that the churchgoing sector of American society is being sorted into increasingly larger churches where they will contribute to shedding those buckets of tears and those billions of dollars. Just how missional all this is remains to be seen. I am now hearing megachurch leaders telling us that their churches are "going missional," a phrase that makes my skin crawl. I agree with Reggie McNeal when he says, "Missional is a way of living, not an affiliation or activity."[9] Other large church leaders have told me defiantly that their churches have always been missional, although my guess is that they really mean they've always been evangelistic. As we'll see later, reducing mission to evangelism is a dead giveaway you haven't quite got hold of the whole missional paradigm. You can't get away with saying you're missional when most of your energy goes chiefly into attracting more attendees, even if your orientation is evangelistic. Evangelism is missional, no question, but it's not all there is to it, and attractional megachurches are being reductionist if they imply or state that winning more converts proves their missionality. But as I said, more on that later.

If America has more megachurches but less churchgoers than ever, we are seeing a worrisome trend. The overall decline in the influence of the church is being masked by the apparent success of these large churches, leading us into a false sense of security. Some people obviously love attending a church with thousands of other attenders, but the bulk of people do not. And it's now questionable whether emerging generations are as taken with the large attractional church as their parents were. In a recent article in the *Dallas Morning News*, cub reporter Clint Rainey wrote, "My generation, the offspring of the megachurch's most loyal fans, isn't quite so gripped."[10] Reacting against the decision by Houston's Lakewood Baptist Church and its celebrity pastor Joel Osteen to spend $75 million to renovate the NBA arena of the Compaq Center, Rainey describes megachurch culture, with all its bells and whistles, as massive and impersonal in every way. A committed Christian who grew up as a member of a megachurch himself, Rainey stresses,

> All of this, we've been reminded interminably, is to "attract seekers." I've grown very disenchanted with this concept. Attract seekers to what? A sanctuary worthy of a Broadway production? An auditorium mimicking a convention center? A complex of expensive buildings? . . . Amid a culture inundated with bigness and cellular technology, iPods and TiVo, the technologized megachurch is no longer impressive.[11]

I once taught a class at the Hillsong College, the leadership training program run by Australia's largest church. I asked the class to raise their hand if they had invited any of their unchurched friends to Hillsong recently, and nearly the whole class raised their hand. I then asked them to raise their hand if any of their friends had decided to become Christians and remain part of the Hillsong congregation. A few students raised their hand. I then asked them to raise their hand if any of their unchurched friends were offended or disturbed or even repulsed by their experience at Hillsong church. Most of them raised their hand, indicating they had some friends who were turned off by the experience. This is hardly extensive research, but it does indicate that while a segment of the population is attracted to the megachurch experience, a much larger segment is repelled by it, including Clint Rainey and his peers. This isn't to dismiss the good work of Hillsong or any other megachurch. It's simply to say we can't expect to put all our eggs in that one basket.

The same could be said of the emerging crop of not-yet-missional alternative churches as well. We can't place all our hopes in any one style of church. Indeed, it is an entirely nonmissional assumption that simply changing the style, tone, or culture of the church will appeal to a new demographic. I have often encountered more resistance to the ideas of the missional paradigm in übercool Gen X–dominated churches than in megachurches. And yet they are both essentially seeking to do the same thing—engineer the church "product" to attract their preferred clientele.

The research I cited earlier suggests that only 17 percent of people looking for spiritual guidance will look for it in a church—that's any church, be it mega, emerging, or anything in between. Commenting on this figure, Neil Cole asks, "Why don't we switch our strategy from attractional church programming to something that empowers and releases Christians to have the real influence?"[12] You see, missional church leaders don't just want to "do church differently." We are not advocating any particular model like simple church, house church, megachurch, seeker-sensitive church, and so on. Missional leaders don't see changing the church as central to their cause; they want to change the whole world. We have been swept up into a new awareness of the *missio Dei*, the unstoppable program of God's unfurling kingdom on earth, and we can't even conceive of how to control it, package it, or franchise it. One cannot be infected by this wonderful life-giving virus and remain content with church-business-as-usual.

And so for those concerned that they might have been inoculated against the missional, I humbly present this small guidebook—a list of indicators that will highlight when the missional paradigm hasn't been fully adopted. I don't mean it as a condemnatory list, but as a positive (perhaps clarion) call for those who have begun to explore the missional but who have resisted its gravitational pull to continue the journey deeper into the risky, but exciting, vortex of the mission of God. To them I say, keep inching along this journey because you have the right concepts in mind and the right language on your tongue, but with all the love and respect in the world, I must say you're *not yet missional*.

And I need to say, *neither am I*. The call to live an incarnational life, to serve as Christ did, and to lead others into the risky vocation of following the missio Dei, is not a simple nor easy task. It is a lifelong calling to service, sacrifice, selflessness, and effort. It will be worked out in neighborhoods and people groups around the world, and fueled and led by the least likely saints. I write not as one who has achieved this perfectly, but as one who has received the missional call from God on my life and who continues to struggle, kick and scream, love and serve my way into a deeper appreciation and adoption of the life to which he has commissioned me. All I can offer are these warnings and correctives to those who sense that they have similarly been called, but who feel the tug to return to church business as usual.

1

THE MISSIO DEI

Seeing Mission as Bigger Than Evangelism

> Despite what people think, within the Christian
> family and outside it, the point of Christianity
> isn't "to go to heaven when you die."
>
> —N. T. Wright

As I mentioned earlier, one of the dead giveaways you're not missional yet is speaking of mission in the same terms that we once used when speaking of evangelism. The argument commonly used is that because we now live in a postmodern/post-Christian/post-church/post-whatever culture, we need to become missional in order to win more people back into our ever-declining churches. What is meant, of course, is that we need to become more evangelistic to attract more converts to our churches. This might well be correct, but applying the term *missional* to the evangelistic enterprise only dilutes the impact of the call to embrace the missional, making it appear that it is just another way of saying get-out-there-and-invite-your-unsaved-friends-to-church, which it is definitely not.

By subverting the missional paradigm into an exclusively evangelistic enterprise, we corrupt its essential logic. And when church leaders read evangelism as a chiefly come-to-us activity, they end up thinking that being missional is just the latest way of being über-attractional. Yet the truly missional energy of the church flows outward as an incarnational impulse. The missional among us are sent ones, profoundly conscious of the commission they have embraced and the community to whom they've been sent.

Alerting People to the Reign of God

David Bosch, the South African missiologist whose work first set me and many others on this missional journey, once wrote, "Mission is more and different from recruitment to our brand of religion; it is the alerting people to the universal reign of God through Christ."[1] And with that he said a mouthful. To reduce mission to the recruitment of new church members is like turning an ox into a bouillon cube. Rather, mission is the most extraordinary cosmic/global activity of "alerting people to the universal reign of God through Christ." For David Bosch and the rest of us who have followed him into this missional paradigm, mission derives from the reign of God. In that respect the ideas of mission and kingdom are irrevocably linked. Mission is both the announcement and the demonstration of the reign of God through Christ. Mission is not primarily concerned with church growth. It is *primarily* concerned with the reign and rule of the Triune God. If the church grows as a result, so be it. Bosch made this clear in his earlier work, *Witness to the World*, as well as his magnum opus, *Transforming Mission*:

> Mission takes place where the church, in its total involvement with the world, bears its testimony in the form of a servant, with reference to unbelief, exploitation, discrimination and violence, but also with reference to salvation, healing, liberation, reconciliation and righteousness.[2]

Mission is not competition with other religions, not a conversion activity, not expanding the faith, not building up the kingdom of God; neither is it social, economic, or political activity. And yet, there is merit in all these projects. So, the church's concern is conversion, church growth, the reign of God, economy, society and politics—but in a different manner![3]

In a different manner, indeed. As I mentioned, the practice and attitude of mission is rooted in a belief in the kingship of the Triune God. God reigns even if not one soul on the face of the earth acknowledges it. His reign is full and complete, an eternal and nonnegotiable reality, not enlarged nor diminished by the number of people who believe it and yield to it. Our mission, then, is to alert people to this irrefutable reality, by both announcement and demonstration. It can never be boiled down to simply giving people information on how to go to heaven when they die. As English bishop and missional pioneer Lesslie Newbigin put it,

The Bible . . . is covered with God's purpose of blessing for all the nations. It is concerned with the completion of God's purpose in the creation of the world. It is not—to put it crudely—concerned with offering a way of escape for the redeemed soul out of history, but with the action of God to bring history to its true end.[4]

This is not some innovative emerging missional approach. Alerting people to the reign of God has always been the essence of the mission of the people of God. As long ago as the book of Isaiah, the exiled people of Israel were being called to "preach the gospel" of Yahweh. One example of Isaiah's use of the word "gospel" is worth quoting. Not only is it a passage directly quoted by a New Testament writer (Rom. 10:15; Eph. 2:17; 6:15), the cluster of words surrounding the gospel-announcement of this passage (peace, salvation, kingdom) are instantly recognizable as important New Testament "gospel" terms and themes. Isaiah 52:7 reads:

How beautiful on the mountains
are the feet of those who bring good news [*basar/
euangelizomai*],

who proclaim peace,
who bring good tidings [*basar/euangelizomai*],
who proclaim salvation,
who say to Zion,
"Your God reigns!"

That's the essence of the mission of Israel, taken up by the follow-ers of Jesus in his new covenant: the alerting of people to the fact that our God reigns. In the New Testament his rule culminates in the death and resurrection of Jesus, but that rule has always been the object of the mission of God's people. As New Testament scholar N. T. Wright explains,

The New Testament picks up from the Old the theme that God in-tends, in the end, to put the whole creation to rights. Earth and heaven were made to overlap with one another, not fitfully, mysteriously, and partially as they do at the moment, but completely, gloriously, and utterly. "The earth shall be filled with the glory of God as the waters cover the sea." That is the promise which resonates throughout the Bible story, from Isaiah (and behind him, by implication, from Gen-esis itself) all the way through to Paul's greatest visionary moments and the final chapters of the book of Revelation. The great drama will end, not with "saved souls" being snatched up into heaven, away from the wicked earth and the mortal bodies which have dragged them down into sin, but with the New Jerusalem coming down from heaven to earth, so that "the dwelling of God is with humans" (Rev. 21:3).[5]

Another way of describing the same idea can be found in Thomas Torrance's *The Christian Frame of Mind*, where the great Scottish professor of theology puts it this way: "In Jesus Christ the new order of the kingdom of God's love has intersected the old order of our existence in this world, with a view to redeeming and liberating it from the forces of disorder and darkness entrenched in it and renew-ing the whole created order."[6]

If mission is this larger, more expansive, more global and history-encompassing enterprise, evangelism is a subset of that larger cat-egory. It is not the sum total of mission. It is *one* of the ways we alert people to the universal reign of God in Christ. In trying to understand the relation between mission and evangelism, David

Bosch identified twelve common historical positions taken by the church. I won't deal with all twelve of them, as some of them have never been in vogue within the mainstream evangelical church. Those that have been adopted to some degree are the first six positions he ennunciates. I have summarized them as follows:

	Mission is . . .	Comments or Cautions
Position 1	Mission = Evangelism = winning souls for eternity	Social involvement is a betrayal of mission.
Position 2	Mission = Evangelism = soul winning	Social action may be good. However, as a rule it distracts from mission and should be discouraged. Social action is optional.
Position 3	Mission/evangelism = soul winning	Social action is important since it may draw people to Christ. Social ministries may act as forerunners to mission. Social action is fine as long as it makes it possible to confront people with the gospel.
Position 4	Mission/evangelism and social involvement relate to each other like seed to fruit.	Evangelism has the primary function of preaching repentance, conversion, and eternal salvation. Social action is the result of such repentance and is therefore secondary.
Position 5	Mission is wider than evangelism. Mission is evangelism plus social action.	Both parts are important, but evangelism has priority.
Position 6	Evangelism and social action are equally important but genuinely distinct aspects of the church's total mission.	We should therefore not prioritize.[7]

Historically the conservative evangelical and fundamentalist movements have long been proponents of Position 1, labeling any social involvement as an expression of the so-called social gospel, and therefore in their minds liberal. However, the new crop of not-yet-missional types are not as hard-line as this and recognize that social action is a legitimate expression of the mission of the church, but they tend to propose something around Positions 2 to 4. For them the primary mission of the church is evangelism. While social action is an expression of the love of God, its chief purpose is for creating a platform for evangelism to occur. Some more progressive evangelicals have been willing to move into Position 5. John Stott and the Lausanne movement would represent this position, acknowledging that evangelism and social action are both elements of the larger mission of the church, but they would want to reaffirm the priority of evangelistic ministry over social action.[8]

I would like to suggest the more distinctly missional approach is to adopt something closer to Position 6, where evangelism and social involvement are so entwined that it is folly to try to unravel them. They are both equally important and equally necessary expressions of this marvelous task of alerting people to the reign of God.

Trying to determine which has priority and which should take precedence is impossible. Some people have tried to force me to make a determination on precedence by inventing some hypothetical situation where I have to imagine myself confronting a starving unbeliever. He will soon die of starvation and enter into a Christless eternity. What would I do, feed him or share Christ with him? The point of the question is to test whether I think a person's greatest need is his or her well-being in this life or salvation in the next. But I think these contrived situations are so far from reality as to make them irrelevant. Life is rarely so neat as to present us with such sharp distinctions between whether to evangelize or to socially engage. If mission is the alerting of people to the reign of God through Christ, our mandate is to do whatever is required in the circumstances to both demonstrate and announce that kingship. We feed the hungry because in the world to come there will be no such thing as starvation. We share Christ because in the world to come there will be no such thing as unbelief. Both are the fashioning of foretastes of that world to come, none more or less valid or important than the other.

It seems to me, then, that a core question for all missional Christians is to ask, what does the reign of God through Christ look like in my neighborhood? If the kingdom of God has come and is overlapping with the broken world in which I live, how can I alert people to it? What does it look like? Where do I see the evidence of it? In fact, it occurs to me that this is a far more legitimate and creative question to ask than the usual questions about how we can attract people to our church programs.

Movie Trailers

One of the ways I've found to respond to these questions is to remind people about the role that film trailers play in cinema. An audience gathers to see a film, but before the feature begins, a series of trailers or previews for upcoming releases is played. Trailers are tasters, short film versions of the soon-to-be-released feature, and they usually include the best special effects or the funniest scenes or the most romantic moments, depending on the film, of the forthcoming feature. Now, watch those around you in the theatre at the end of each trailer. If it has done its job, usually one person will turn to the other and say, "I want to see that movie."

This is a great metaphor for the missional church. If it does its job well, people will see what it does and say, "I want to see the world they come from." Far from being a cute illustration, this is at the very core of Christian mission. The church is to be like a trailer for the New Jerusalem, a taster, with all the best bits on full display. If we conclude that the world to come will be a place of complete and perfect justice, it follows that the mission of the church is to create foretastes of the justice to come. Likewise, if we believe that the world to come is a place of love and mercy, we are to be a trailer of that love and mercy, a free sample for those looking to buy into the whole thing. Read the Scriptures and compile a picture of the world to come—justice, love, peace, reconciliation—and then go forth to fashion foretastes of that world. But, of course, if we believe that in the New Jerusalem "every knee should bow . . . and every tongue confess that Jesus Christ is Lord" (Phil. 2:10–11), our mission is to create foretastes of such worship by encouraging belief where there is currently unbelief. In this way we both demonstrate and announce the reign of God through Christ.

There is no longer any need to debate whether we prefer evangelism or social justice. There is no longer any need to argue about which is primary and which creates a platform for the other. This concern about hierarchy is redundant. We should not be committed to social action purely as a means to create opportunities to do the "real mission" of evangelism. Not only do non-Christians see this manipulative ploy a mile off, it is biblically screwy anyway. We are called to alert people to the reign and rule of God through Christ, and this will involve being trailers that both demonstrate (justice, love, reconciliation) and announce (heralding, worship, evangelism) that reign.

The metaphor Paul uses that best equates with trailers is that of *firstfruits*. This quaint term appears throughout the Old Testament and refers to the first portion of the annual harvest that is given to God. Most notably the firstfruits were dedicated to God in the hope of a greater harvest to follow. They were seen as a kind of down payment from God, the taste of things to come from the gracious hand of Yahweh. But when Paul employs the term in his letter to the Romans, he is referring to the presence of the Spirit, the in-breaking of the kingdom of heaven here on earth. He says,

> The creation waits in eager expectation for the sons of God to be revealed. For the creation was subjected to frustration, not by its own choice, but by the will of the one who subjected it, in hope that the creation itself will be liberated from its bondage to decay and brought into the glorious freedom of the children of God. We know that the whole creation has been groaning as in the pains of childbirth right up to the present time. Not only so, but we ourselves, who have the firstfruits of the Spirit, groan inwardly as we wait eagerly for our adoption as sons, the redemption of our bodies. For in this hope we were saved. But hope that is seen is no hope at all. Who hopes for what he already has? But if we hope for what we do not yet have, we wait for it patiently. (Rom. 8:19–25)

For Paul, the Christian community has received this firstfruits of the Spirit, the down payment or foretaste of the world to come, and in the reception of such a gift, he believes the Christian community, like all of creation, will groan with eager expectation of the full payment, the final transaction, the complete appearing of the glory of God. As we noted earlier in the words of N. T. Wright, this appearance of heaven on earth will be complete, glorious, and total, but at the moment it overlaps "fitfully, mysteriously, and partially." And for Paul this is the source of his frustration. He yearns deeply for the completion of the age, and groans with expectation as he sees the fitful, partial evidence of that day.

The missional outworking of this metaphor is that we, the Christian community, are to behave like the firstfruits, like the harvest that is to come. Imagine a first-century farmer surveying his fields at the end of winter and seeing the first buds of life, the first green shoots, the nascent presence of fruit. These first indications of the crop that he will harvest in spring bring renewed hope after the darkness of winter. They are the equivalent of a movie trailer—the best scenes, the funniest lines, the biggest explosions of the full upcoming feature. But note that Paul points out that the whole creation groans with us. The very planet yearns for renewal. It joins us in that chorus of expectation. Just as snow-capped mountains and raging rivers and lush fields are reminders or foretastes of the renewed planet to come, so should our communities of faith, hope, and love be similar examples of the shape of things to come. Lesslie Newbigin sums it up this way:

> We do indeed look forward with eager longing to that Christian society which is the final goal of all God's creative and redemptive love, but until that day we are called upon to seek on earth a society which, as far as may be granted to us, reflects the glory of the city to which we look forward.[9]

The Feast of Epiphany

To return to David Bosch, he was one of the first to sound a warning that by limiting mission to evangelistic technique, the church would end up with a reductionist approach to mission that emphasizes strategy and technique over and above a broader desire to cooperate with the missionary God in his totality. Bosch is often quoted as saying that the church is not to "undertake" mission but to be constituted by the missio Dei.[10] This isn't to disregard the missionary activities of the church (referred to by Bosch as the *missiones ecclesiae*) but they must be allowed to be subsumed by the missio Dei. He wrote,

> The primary purpose of the *missiones ecclesiae* can therefore not simply be the planting of churches or the saving of souls; rather it has to be service to the *missio Dei*, representing God in and over against the world in a ceaseless celebration of the Feast of the Epiphany.[11]

This might appear to be a subtle distinction, but in fact what he is describing is a yawning canyon of difference. He is suggesting that rather than boiling mission down to an assortment of missionary activities, the church should step into its calling to alert people to the reign of God through Christ and allow ministries, strategies, or goal-setting to emerge as a result of that grander vocation.

The Feast of the Epiphany is, of course, a Christian festival, observed on January 6, commemorating the manifestation of Christ to the Gentiles in the persons of the Magi. But what Bosch is suggesting is that such a festival ought to be the everyday experience of the church. The celebration of the coming of heaven to earth and the offer of citizenship to all people, Jew or Gentile, should epitomize both our corporate life-together and our missional life-for-others. Mission therefore should be something like an endless party. It is characterized by celebration, joy, relief. Note how Paul describes this very feeling:

> For we ourselves were once foolish, disobedient, led astray, slaves to various passions and pleasures, passing our days in malice and envy, despicable, hating one another. But when the goodness and loving kindness of God our Savior appeared, he saved us, not because of any works of righteousness that we had done, but according to his mercy, through the water of rebirth and renewal by the Holy Spirit. (Titus 3:3–5 NRSV)

You can almost hear the relief. Note especially the method of entry into the endless celebration of the Feast of the Epiphany—regeneration (water of rebirth) and renewal (by the Spirit). It is obvious there is a strong resonance with Jesus' mysterious words to Nicodemus: "I tell you the truth, no one can enter the kingdom of God unless he is born of water and the Spirit" (John 3:5). The means of admission to the endless feast is via water and the Spirit—regeneration and renewal. We are remade, reshaped, and reborn, and the result is that we are fit for celebration. To return to Paul's earlier metaphor, we have received the firstfruits. And while we groan for the full harvest, we have also entered into a world where, like wide-eyed children, we spend our days in astonishment at the unfurling of the world to come all around us. Not to labor the point, but such a vision is as old as the words of the prophet Ezekiel forecasting what it will be like on the day of the Lord:

I will sprinkle clean water upon you, and you shall be clean from all your uncleannesses, and from all your idols I will cleanse you. A new heart I will give you and a new spirit I will put within you; and I will remove from your body the heart of stone and give you a heart of flesh. I will put my spirit within you, and make you follow my statutes and be careful to observe my ordinances. (Ezek. 36:25–27 NRSV)

Jesus' and Paul's references to personal regeneration and renewal are music to the ears of those who believe our mission is entirely evangelistic. But what helps broaden our understanding of mission is the allusion Jesus makes to his triumphant return when he tells his disciples, "Truly I tell you, at the renewal of all things, when the Son of Man is seated on the throne of his glory, you who have followed me will also sit on twelve thrones, judging the twelve tribes of Israel" (Matt. 19:28 NRSV). That phrase, "at the renewal of all things," derives from the Greek word *palingenesia*. This word appears only twice in the whole New Testament. The other time is in the Titus passage we just looked at where it is translated as "water of rebirth" (Titus 3:5 NRSV). In older translations it appeared as "regeneration." When Paul uses the term "regeneration" in that passage, he does so in relation to the rebirth of individuals. But when Jesus employs the same term in Matthew 19, he is referring to the rebirth or regeneration of "all things."

There is no disagreement here between Paul and Jesus. We have already seen Paul speaking of the whole of creation groaning for its final and complete redemption. And we have heard Jesus telling Nicodemus that he, an individual, must be reborn by water and the Spirit. The point is, the New Testament teaches that in Christ the Feast of Epiphany has been inaugurated and the whole of the planet is invited, Jew and Gentile, humanity and creation. Tim Keller, the pastor of Redeemer Presbyterian Church in New York City, describes it this way: "The Gospel is the good news that God himself has come to rescue and renew all of creation through the work of Jesus Christ on our behalf."[12] Amen!

Therefore, every act of alerting people to the universal reign of God through Christ is an act of worship and of celebration. We celebrate every warm spring breeze because it reminds us of the order of things, the way things are meant to be, the way things will one day always be. We are drawn to beautiful sunsets and sunrises, magnificent mountain ranges, and white sandy beaches precisely because they offer us traces of a world renewed, foretastes of the world to come. They provide hope that tsunamis and earthquakes and drought and melting polar ice are not the final word. We should feast on these foretastes of the coming world. In the same way, moments of love and grace, acts of justice and peacemaking, are a scent of the society to come. They should be noticed, savored, and enjoyed by those of us who have entered into the endless Feast of the Epiphany, for they too are examples of the reign and rule of God in Christ, unfurling across the world-as-it-is, pointing to the world-to-come.

Chris Seay from the Ecclesia community in Houston told me of a wonderful way to remain mindful in celebrating the endless Feast of the Epiphany, particularly with children. He has taught his children to identify examples of *shalom*—the dream of God for human society and his creation. Although directly translated into English as "peace," shalom doesn't simply refer to an absence of conflict or inner personal calm. It refers to that dream of *rightness*, the regeneration of all things of which Jesus spoke. It includes inner peace and global peace, but also prosperity, justice, wellness, and reconciliation. When we look for examples of shalom, we are sniffing out the scent of the kingdom, the reign and rule of God through Christ. Chris has taught his children to look at the scenes of their lives and see examples of God's reign or the yearning for that reign. For example, when they see someone feeding the poor, the Seay kids identify it is as whiff of shalom. But when they see a filthy, unkempt homeless person panhandling on a street corner, Chris has taught them to see it as *broken shalom*. It reveals the yearning for home and warmth and love, but it is broken—a cracked example of what could be and should be. In this way, Chris is teaching his children not only to celebrate the presence of God's reign but also to hunger for more of it, and presumably to cooperate with God to work toward seeing more of that reign.

Looking for shalom and broken shalom is a brilliant example of, to reuse Bosch's phrase, the ceaseless celebration of the Feast of the Epiphany. It is a way to identify and celebrate what God is doing and how his rule is being seen. If you've ever taken children to the zoo or a fair or a theme park, you've probably seen them running hither and yon, pointing at each attraction with ever increasing excitement. Their oohs and aahs betray their unchecked joy at spying out each new ride or wild animal. This is what the Feast of the Epiphany could be like—Jesus' followers celebrating like children at their unfolding awareness of God's reign and rule and then getting on board for the ride of their lives. This will lead to the inevitable desire to serve our communities in need and provide the services that demonstrate the kingdom of God to those who may be experiencing a sense of displacement in the kingdom of the world. As Scottish theologian Thomas Torrance says,

> It is incumbent upon us, therefore, to relate the *actual order* we find in the world to the *redemptive order* which lies at the heart of the Christian message. In the Christian faith we look for a *new order* in which the *damaged order*, or the disorder that inexplicably arises in the world, will be healed through a *creative reordering* of existence as it is reconciled to its ultimate ground in the creative love of God.[13]

And we should continue to exalt this kind of identification and celebration as gospel work. To diminish it as somehow inferior to the so-called real mission of evangelism only devalues both the activity and the work of evangelism. As I've noted, and will detail at greater length in the next chapter, the gospel is much, much more than giving people information on having a happier afterlife. It is, to reiterate, alerting people to the universal reign of God through Christ by both announcement and demonstration. Scot McKnight, New Testament scholar and popular author, summarizes it this way: "The Gospel is the work of God to restore humans to union with God and communion with others, in the context of a community for the good of others and the world."[14]

Finding Thin Places

As I've stated, there's no reason why this more expansive definition of mission should exclude personal witness and faith-sharing. Since the core project of the mission of the church is alerting people to the reign of God in Christ, it can be done with the lips (evangelism, personal witness, worship) and with the hands (serving, healing, caring), with neither one becoming secondary to the other. In this way, enjoying a good cup of fair-trade coffee at your local coffee shop might be a minuscule example of cooperating with the mission of God, but it's certainly not all there is to it. We can't fall into the trap of imagining everything we want to do is necessarily mission. As has been stated before, if everything is mission, nothing is mission. While the large church pastors might have minimized the *demonstration* aspect of mission, some of the emerging leaders can just as equally minimize the *announcement* aspect of mission.

The Celts speak of "thin places," where the fabric that separates heaven and earth is so thin it becomes almost translucent and one is able to encounter the joy and peace of heaven. In the Celtic tradition, such places give us an opening into the magnificence and wonder of the world to come. There is a Celtic saying that heaven and earth are only three feet apart, but in the thin places that distance is even smaller. To them a thin place is where the veil that separates heaven and earth is lifted and one is able to receive a glimpse of the glory of God. It is no wonder that thin places are most often associated with wild landscapes. A thin place requires us to step from one world to another, and for many pilgrims that often means traveling to a place where we have less control and where the unpredictable becomes the means of discovery. Rugged seacoast like the Cliffs of St. David's, windswept islands like Iona, and rocky mountain peaks like Croagh Patrick were thin places in ancient times and still call out to pilgrims today.

Yet I want to dare us to find thin places in our everyday lives, to search out those times and places where we see God's new order of things breaking through, despite the disorder of our current experience, and to cooperate with them, teasing them out for others to see. When Jesus said, "Whatever you did for one of the least of these brothers of mine, you did for me" (Matt. 25:40), he was referring to something not unlike the Celts' idea of a thin place. It is a place where we cooperate so fully with the reign of God in Christ that this reign breaks through into the disorder of poverty and hunger. Likewise, when Jesus said to Nicodemus, "I tell you the truth, no one can see the kingdom of God unless he is born again" (John 3:3), he was also speaking of a place where the kingdom of order and faith breaks through into this world of disorder and faithlessness.

A new birth occurs. The veil is lifted and we are born into a whole new order of things. Jesus then describes this thin place further:

> I tell you the truth, no one can enter the kingdom of God unless he is born of water and the Spirit. Flesh gives birth to flesh, but the Spirit gives birth to spirit. You should not be surprised at my saying, "You must be born again." The wind blows wherever it pleases. You hear its sound, but you cannot tell where it comes from or where it is going. So it is with everyone born of the Spirit. (John 3:5–8)

Nicodemus stands at that thin place, where the veil that separates heaven and earth is nearly translucent, and he is on the verge of entering a whole new world like a newborn baby. Thin places are those moments in time and space when we are alerted afresh to the reign of God through Christ. They can occur when that reign is enacted or demonstrated by acts of kindness, love, and mercy, or when that reign is announced in no uncertain terms, evoking faith, worship, and repentance. Thin places occur in soup kitchens, AIDS clinics, community gardens, and crisis housing units as well as in church buildings and monasteries.

Thin places can occur in the everyday-ness of life as well. We encounter something of the world as it should be in a beautiful piece of music or a stunning piece of art. Sometimes a scene in a film can take us by surprise and open our eyes to the reign of God. Often these thin places can occur in moments of unguarded intimacy and hospitality shared between friends or spouses. Acts of generosity and mercy can invite the recipient into such a thin place.

It needs to be pointed out again, for the purposes of clarity, that while these might be useful indicators, they do not themselves constitute mission. The church is to be subsumed by the missio Dei. The church must not believe that its activity alone is the mission. As Newbigin so forcefully points out, the church needs to recover an eschatology that recognizes that our political or religious activity cannot establish the kingdom of God. Rather, a belief that the coming reign of God is the framework for all missionary practice.

If we feed the hungry or preach the gospel, we do so as an act of worship, as part of our ceaseless celebration of the Feast of the Epiphany, in response to the lordship of the Triune God. While this certainly has political, social, and ecclesial implications, it isn't in itself an expression of politics, society, or church. It is our automatic response to God's reign and rule, proven through Christ, revealed through the Spirit. Therefore, any collective of believers set free from the disorder of this present age, who offer themselves in service of the mission of their God to alert people to the new unfolding order of things, can rightly be called a missional church. One of the early Newbiginian thinkers in the US, Lois Barrett, defined the missional church as such:

> A church that is shaped by participating in God's mission, which is to set things right in a broken, sinful world, to redeem it, and restore it to what God has always intended for the world. Missional churches see themselves not so much sending, as being sent. A missional congregation lets God's mission permeate everything that the congregation does—from worship to witness to training members for discipleship. It bridges the gap between outreach and congregational life, since, in its life together, the church is to embody God's mission.[15]

A few years ago I met Pastor Abraham Hang at a leadership conference in Phnom Penh. We stood on a balcony overlooking the brown-colored Tonle Sap River that flows through the city toward the Mekong. On previous visits I had noticed the hundreds of squatter huts that had been erected on the steep riverbank, corrugated iron shacks perched precariously on bamboo stilts above the river that rises so dramatically during the monsoon season. Now, they are all gone, demolished by the military, their residents evicted to swampland outside the city limits. Abraham and his wife moved to that resettlement village at Andong and began the lifelong process of joining the mission of God in that place among the poorest people in one of the poorest nations on earth.

When I asked him how he got started, he told me he simply asked the Lord what he should do to create foretastes of the world to come among the poverty and desperation of Andong Resettlement Village. The Lord told him to dry out the muddy swamp underfoot, a breeding ground for mosquitoes and disease. And so Abraham, together with the men of the village, and helped by Christian men from around about, dug deep trenches to drain away the water left during the wet season to dry out the land and make life more bearable.

Then he arranged for Christian doctors and dentists to bring mobile clinics to Andong, believing as he did that in the world to come there will be no sickness or disease. Then he started a preschool and a school. Then, because so many people had come to trust in Jesus, Abraham's God, he started a church in the slum. Then he found the funding through a local missionary to build hundreds of thatch-roof houses because he was convinced that in the world to come no one will live under corrugated iron in temperatures of 100 degrees and 100 percent humidity. Then, because public transportation costs made it prohibitive for the men of the village to get into the city to look for day jobs as menial laborers, Abraham raised the money to buy a truck in order to drive them there and back each morning and evening.

I walked through narrow and winding streets of Andong with Abraham one day, struggling with the heat and flies, but amazed by the transformation that the gospel had brought to that place. As we wandered these streets, residents would appear, and with their hands together before their faces in the traditional Cambodian greeting, they would begin to speak to me unprompted and enthusiastically in Khmer, which I can't understand. Abraham felt obliged to translate as he sheepishly reported that they were telling me about the change that had occurred in their lives since they had come to accept the universal reign of God through Christ. His embarrassment was due to the fact that his neighbors were praising God for sending Abraham to their village. Later we sat on the bamboo slat floor of a corrugated-iron coffee shop in the slum, and we talked more about the ways that the lordship of Jesus was being both announced and demonstrated in Andong.

I was so impressed, I asked Abraham about where he had learned about this new missional paradigm here in Cambodia. Not fully understanding my question, he asked me to repeat myself, so I simplified it: what books have you read that have shaped your thinking about mission?

Abraham thought awhile and then nodded. He understood the question this time. "Matthew, Luke, the Acts of the Apostles . . ."

SLOW EVANGELISM

Moving Beyond the Four Spiritual Laws

> The best hermeneutic of the Gospel is a com-
> munity of men and women who believe it and
> live by it.
>
> —Lesslie Newbigin

Some years ago I heard well-known writer and speaker Brian McLaren attempting to recast the way the church perceives evangelism. He rather cheekily presented the following caricature of the contemporary gospel, preached faithfully from pulpits across the world, using slides of decreasing font size until the final line was so minuscule it could barely be read:

Primarily information on how to go to heaven after you die . . .

with a large footnote about increasing your personal happiness
and success through God . . .

with a small footnote about character development . . .

with a smaller footnote about spiritual experience . . .

with an even smaller footnote about social/global transformation.

While it is a caricature, I think it reveals an awkward truth: When
the contemporary evangelical church tries to present what it believes is the core message of the Bible, it nearly always does so in
individualized terms, and it nearly always does so by presenting the
message of Jesus as being about personalized benefit either in this
world or the next. And yet, as we've seen, the gospel as presented
in the New Testament, and its precursor in the Old Testament, is
anchored in the reign of God through Christ and the unfolding
personal, social, and global transformation that it promises. In
this vein, in *More Ready Than You Realize*, Brian McLaren offers
a guide to evangelism, based on the true story of how he interacted
with a postmodern seeker via email. He describes the differences
between the old, outdated modernist approach and a newer, more
postmodern approach:

> **Out:** Evangelism as sales pitch, as conquest, as warfare, as ultima-
> tum, as threat, as proof, as argument, as entertainment, as show, as
> monologue, as something you have to do.

> **In:** Disciple-making as conversation, as friendship, as influence, as
> invitation, as companionship, as challenge, as opportunity, as dance,
> as something you get to do.[1]

Brian is also extensively quoted on this distinction between gaining converts and making disciples in Dan Kimball's *The Emerging
Church*, especially in chapter 18, "Evangelism: Beyond the Prayer
to Get into Heaven."[2] Alan Hirsch and I have said similar things
about the tone and nature of evangelism.[3] There seems to be a growing awareness that the old "sales pitch" approach to evangelism,

where the evangelizer buttonholes a potential convert and takes him or her through a prepared screed like "The Four Spiritual Laws" is less authentic these days and therefore less effective. Younger Christians are gun-shy of such approaches and have turned away from them in droves, which has led some church leaders to decry these Christians as "liberal" or wishy-washy in their faith. And it is certainly true that a great many churches that would identify themselves as emerging missional churches are rather sluggish in their growth in numbers and reticent to talk about the incidence of "conversions" in their community. Mark Driscoll has commented on what he sees to be the poor conversion growth of the emerging churches in the US.[4] Recent criticism of emerging church leaders' views on the atonement have raised questions about how seriously the emerging church takes conventional evangelism.[5] By emphasizing discipleship so broadly, do we risk losing any call to conversion? Surely, if mission is about alerting people to the reign of God through Christ, the announcement of that reign—the articulated declaration of the lordship of Jesus—needs to have a central place. Those who claim to be missional but who never ever find themselves in a relational place where they can proclaim the lordship of Jesus to a friend, even if that proclamation occurs over several conversations over a period of time, are hardly missional at all. I get tired of people telling me that they concur with St. Francis of Assisi, who was claimed to have said, "Preach the gospel at all times, and use words if necessary." I happen to agree with the assumption behind this Franciscan maxim, but those who are most inclined to quote it to me these days are those least inclined to find it necessary to ever use words when preaching the gospel.

So, it seems we are divided between gung-ho types who will happily flash their gospel tracts like a US marshal flashing his badge, and the emerging generation of young adult Christians who are reticent to let the name of Jesus pass their lips without coming off like a nutty fundamentalist. To be fair, a lot of young Christians I know are eager to be evangelistically engaged, but the only paradigm they have is the old "hit 'em with the Four Spiritual Laws" approach, and they just can't go there. There seems to be a desperate need for a new, more missional understanding of evangelism that doesn't turn us into foot soldiers or religious telemarketers.

What Exactly Is Evangelism?

As I've already stated, the mission of God is far wider than the evangelistic enterprise. Indeed, evangelism is *one* of the aspects or functions of the missio Dei, but not the only one. We alert people to God's reign through Christ in a variety of ways, one of which is the verbal announcement of that reign. We must see evangelism in this broader context. But, having said that, we need to be careful not to assume that unexplained action is evangelistic. As it's used in the New Testament, the term *evangelism* describes a verbal announcement. It is a declarative activity. Words are required. As David Bosch points out, "This message is indeed necessary. It is unique. It cannot be replaced by unexplained deeds."[6] But as Bosch also pointed out, there is no perfect set of words that captures the gospel, and it is ludicrous to think that we can train Christians to present the gospel as a five-minute sales pitch.

Part of the problem with evangelism is many Christians feel they need to get the whole gospel out in one conversation. The reason for this is many Christians are only ever in a position to "evangelize" strangers, because all their friends are Christians. When the only "evangelism" we do is with strangers on airplanes or at dinner parties or business conferences, we feel an understandable pressure to get all the bases covered, because this might be the only opportunity we (or they) get. Evangelizing friends and neighbors, gradually, relationally, over an extended time, means that the breadth and beauty of the gospel can be expressed slowly without the urgency of the one-off pitch.

When we understand what it is to be truly missional—incarnated deeply within a local host community—we will find that evangelism is best done slowly, deliberately, in the context of a loving community. It takes time and multiple engagements. It requires the unbeliever to observe our lifestyle, see our demonstrations of the reign of God, test our values, enjoy our hospitality. And it must occur as a communal activity, not only as a solo venture. Unbelievers must see the nature and quality of the embodied gospel in community. And all the while, conversations, questions, discussions, and even debates occur wherein we can verbally express our devotion to the reign of God through Christ. No more billboards. No more television commercials. No more unsolicited mail. If evangelism is like a meal, think of it as being prepared in a slow cooker and served over a long night around a large table. It can't be microwaved. It can't be takeout.

In 1986, Italian chef and provedore Carlo Petrini founded the Slow Food movement which has since expanded globally to over 100,000 members in 132 countries. Slow Food exists to "counteract fast food and fast life, the disappearance of local food traditions and people's dwindling interest in the food they eat, where it comes from, how it tastes and how our food choices affect the rest of the world. To do that, Slow Food brings together pleasure and responsibility, and makes them inseparable."[7]

Well, that's what missional thinkers are attempting to do with evangelism—to slow it down, to counteract the abuses of fast evangelism, to place evangelism back into community, to rediscover both the pleasure and the responsibility of announcing the reign of God. It shouldn't be a one-off, hit-or-miss presentation. As Bryan Stone from Boston University points out, it is as messy and organic and communal as life itself:

> The practice of evangelism is a complex and multilayered process—a context of multiple activities that invite, herald, welcome, and provoke and that has as its end the peaceable reign of God and the social holiness by which persons are oriented to that reign.[8]

Part of the problem is that so many of our models for evangelism are itinerant evangelists and pastors. These people rarely tell stories about being deeply incarnated into a neighborhood or host community. Rather, their examples are all about "evangelizing" strangers on airplanes. They tell us about how they managed to fashion just the right line at the perfect time that broke their subject open and allowed them to present Christ to them. They make these presentations to people they will never see again and for whom they feel no sense of ongoing responsibility. It is the equivalent of fast-food evangelism, and it's not the way it was meant to be.

So, how is it meant to be? What exactly is evangelism? David Bosch defines it:

> Evangelism is that dimension and activity of the church's mission which, by word and deed and in light of particular conditions and a

particular context, offers every person and community, everywhere, a valid opportunity to be directly challenged to a radical reorientation of their lives.[9]

Since Bosch managed to pack a series of ideas into that one sentence, we need to do a bit of unpacking. We could parse his definition in the following way:

a. evangelism is a dimension of mission, not its sum total;
b. evangelism is part of the *church's* mission, not just an activity for individuals;
c. evangelism involves both word and deed;
d. evangelism occurs within, and is influenced by, certain cultural and relational conditions and in a certain context;
e. evangelism challenges people to a *radical reorientation* of their lives.

Sharing your faith with a stranger on a plane or some other form of public transportation is not a bad thing as such, particularly if the conversation veers in that direction. But it is not an exemplar of the things mentioned above. It is a solo activity, conducted between virtual strangers, outside of their particular cultural contexts, and if "successful" it leaves the evangelized having prayed some sinner's prayer that will guarantee them eternal salvation. Where's the church community? Where's the shared context? Where's both word and deed? And, above all, where is the radical reorientation of which Bosch speaks?

That radical reorientation should of course involve the decision to acknowledge the reign of God through Christ and submit oneself to live under it. It is more than saying a prayer that will provide you with the golden ticket into heaven when you die. It is the breathtaking and foolhardy risk to live every day under the assumption that the Triune God does indeed reign. Bosch went on to describe the outworkings of this reorientation, involving as it does such things as:

- deliverance from slavery to the world and its powers
- embracing Christ as Savior and Lord
- becoming a living member of Christ's community, the church

- being enlisted into his service of reconciliation, peace, and justice on earth
- being committed to God's purpose of placing all things under the rule of Christ[10]

Presenting the Gospel

If the mission of the church is the alerting of people to the reign of God through Christ, then it follows that those who reorient their lives to God would be committed to God's purpose of placing all things under the rule of Christ. This is a core expression of faith in the biblical God, and it rarely finds itself in any of the church's favorite tracts or gospel presentations. Until recently, the missional responsibility of the believer was never mentioned in evangelistic presentations. One exception to this is the recent InterVarsity presentation *The Big Story*, sometimes referred to as the four circles because it involves retelling the gospel in four stages, each one represented by a circle. It was designed by IVP director James Choung, and its four stages are

1. **Designed for Good**—affirming that the world was created as a good, wonderful place where everything was right with each other;
2. **Damaged by Evil**—describing the presence of sin and brokenness in this world, both personal and global;
3. **Restored for Better**—outlining the atonement of Jesus and its power in bringing God and humankind back into relationship with each other; and
4. **Sent Together to Heal**—commissioning believers, with the power of the Spirit and the community of God's people, to be sent out together to heal the planet.[11]

Stages (or circles) 1 to 3 are not that different from many similar tracts or rote presentations, but it's the presence of the fourth circle—commissioning new believers into the service of the kingdom of God—that sets it apart and reveals the emerging recognition of the ethical implications of the gospel. Evangelism then is more than a discussion about human sin and existential yearning and how Jesus can alleviate them. It is the announcement of God's reign through Christ and an invitation to live under that rule, to place all things under the lordship of the Triune God. This has enormous personal, local, and global ramifications.

More recently, David Benson, a friend of mine from Brisbane, Australia, has added a fifth stage (or circle) to James Choung's original design (with permission). Calling his presentation *Epic Story*, David's fifth circle is called **Set Everything Right**, and he describes it this way:

> For all our best efforts we're still broken. By ourselves, the world will never fully heal. [God] is patient and wants everyone to freely choose the role we were made for. But the day is coming when Jesus will return, judge the world, and set everything right.[12]

This, of course, sounds the eschatological note that Lesslie Newbigin cautioned us earlier not to forget, that a belief in the coming reign of God is the framework for all missionary practice. While we do call people to follow Jesus and be sent together to heal a broken world, we remain conscious that it is ultimately Jesus' work to set everything right.

This is as it was seen in the beginning by the first evangelists. When they "preached the gospel," it was never as a condemnatory presentation about human sin. It was always anchored in the historical fact of the Jesus event and its significance for humankind. In the previous chapter I noted the link between the Old Testament use of the term *basar* and the New Testament references to *euangelizomai*. There are very good reasons for believing that the latter derives in no small measure from the former, and in particular, from Isaiah 40–66, where in 40:9; 41:27; 52:7; and 61:1, the word "evangelize" (tell the gospel) appears several times (in Hebrew, it is *basar*; in Greek, it is *euangelizomai*). An analysis of their respective usages reveals a striking level of correspondence between the New Testament and Isaiah's use of this word. Furthermore, on several occasions the New Testament directly quotes and/or alludes to passages in Isaiah that contain the "gospel" word (for example, Matt. 11:5; Mark 1:14–15; Luke 4:18; Luke 7:22; Acts 10:36; Rom. 10:15; and Eph. 2:17).

To cut a long exegetical story short, from the five passages in which "gospel" appears in Isaiah (40:1–11; 52:1–10; 60:1–7; 61:1–3), one of which I quoted in the previous chapter, the following conclusions may be drawn:

1. *Important News*: The simple stem *angel* denotes a message, messenger, or reporting of a message. When the stem is prefixed by *eu-*, this essential meaning does not change. However, an air of importance appears to attach itself to the stem when the prefix appears. This importance may relate to the inherent goodness of the message, or perhaps the joy the message produces. But this is complicated by evidence elsewhere in the Old Testament which appears to suggest that "gospel" did not always denote good news. For example, in David's lament over the deaths of Saul and Jonathan the king forbids a public proclamation (*basar/euangelizomai*—2 Sam. 1:20) of the tragic events. See also 2 Samuel 18:27. In view of this, it is better to understand the prefix *eu-* (in relation to *angelion*) as primarily denoting importance rather than goodness. The fact that the adverb *eu* on its own can mean "greatly" or "abundantly" supports this. The New Testament also uses *euangelion* in a way that clearly does not mean good news—Romans 2:16; Revelation 14:6.
2. *News of Events*: In every instance in which the word appears in Isaiah, the "gospel" announced is a report of events that are to occur in history—the gathering of God's exiled people, victory over foreign enemies, exaltation of the Jerusalem temple, and so forth. It is not like the word "teach" or "dialogue," which refer more to the communication of ideas. This is consistently borne out in the Greco-Roman usage of the term as well, where it may refer to the announcement of a birth of a child, a military victory, a marriage, etc. The word "gospel" is very much like the modern media term "news flash."
3. *News of Salvation*: The words and ideas of "salvation" are always attached to Isaiah's use of *euangelion*. God as the rescuer of his people is at the core of the term's connotations.
4. *News of God's Rule*: At every point, the important news of the events relating to God's salvation are framed in the context

and language of God's kingship over the world. In Isaiah 52:7, for instance, the precise content of the gospel proclamation is "Your God rules as King!"

5. *News about the Future*: In each of the Isaianic passages in which *euangel-* appears, the announcement is eschatological. That is, it concerns the coming reign of God in which he will reverse the fortunes of his oppressed and condemned people. This eschatological connotation is an important feature of the New Testament use of the term "gospel," in which the idea of fulfillment appears to be significant. I am thinking specifically of Mark 1:15 ("the time is fulfilled, and the kingdom of God is at hand; repent and believe in the gospel" [ESV]) and Romans 1:2ff. ("the gospel of God, which he promised beforehand through his prophets in the holy Scriptures" [ESV]).

My point in all this comparison is to suggest that the gospel, as it was understood by the earliest evangelists, was not simply about a four-point presentation of certain doctrines, particularly those about human sin and the atonement. I'm not suggesting these doctrines weren't important, but I believe the earliest evangelists, influenced as they were by the Isaianic usage of *basar*, saw evangelism as the announcement of an event, the description of a salvation-bringing event in history—the incarnation, the death, and the resurrection of Jesus. They were more concerned with announcing the Jesus event than they were with detailed descriptions of doctrinal belief. In many old-school "gospel presentations," Jesus only appears toward the end of the presentation, the answer to the dilemmas raised in the early phase of the presentation. But Jesus isn't point four of a five-point presentation. Jesus *is* the gospel. At least that's how the earliest evangelists saw it.

The Gospel according to Paul

Take Paul, for example. If we explore Paul's understanding of the gospel, you might be surprised it isn't full of detailed explanations of the doctrine of justification by faith. It is all about the Jesus event, notwithstanding his marvelous explanation of justification by faith in Romans 3:21–26. But that passage isn't an evangelistic treatise. In Romans 3 Paul is reminding the Romans of the meaning of the cross, not preaching the gospel to them. When we turn to all those passages that explicitly reveal the content of the apostle's missionary *kērygma*, or preaching, we find something slightly but importantly different. Let's look for those places where Paul self-consciously reminds his readers of the "gospel."

While Romans 3:21–26 does not fit this above criterion, two other passages in Romans do. In the opening verses of the letter, Paul provides for his readers a summary of the "gospel of God." In what scholars hold to be an early creedal formula known to both Paul and the Roman congregations, the apostle writes:

> Paul, a servant of Christ Jesus, called to be an apostle and set apart for the gospel of God—the gospel he promised beforehand through his prophets in the Holy Scriptures regarding his Son, who as to his human nature was a descendant of David, and who through the Spirit of holiness was declared with power to be the Son of God by his resurrection from the dead: Jesus Christ our Lord. (Rom. 1:1–4)

Here is Paul's gospel, and it is almost entirely news about the historical event of the incarnation and the resurrection as foretold by the prophets in the Holy Writings. It is about his Son, who, being a physical descendant of David, was installed as the mighty Son of God according to the Spirit of holiness from the moment of his resurrection from the dead. He is Messiah Jesus, our Lord. For Paul, the "gospel" consists of a proclamation of Jesus and his messianic credentials: his physical descent from King David, his vindication/validation by the Spirit of God, and his resurrection from the dead. This looks very much like the "gospel" given to us in Matthew's Gospel, with its focus on the kingly rule of Jesus as displayed in his birth, life, death, and resurrection. And note how the emphasis is on historic events rather than systematic theological ideas. As Peter Stuhlmacher writes concerning this passage: "Verses 3 and 4 contain the history of Christ told in the Gospels in short form, and emphasize that the entire way of Jesus, from his birth to his exaltation, stands under the sign of the promises of God."[13]

Later in Romans, Paul offers an even briefer summary of the missionary message. Romans 10:8–9 reads: "But what does it say? 'The word is near you; it is in your mouth and in your heart,' that is, the word of faith we are proclaiming: That if you confess with your mouth, 'Jesus is Lord,' and believe in your heart that God raised him from the dead, you will be saved."

This is like the *Reader's Digest* version of the Romans 1 passage, distilling the Jesus event down to its core essentials: his lordship and his resurrection. Paul indicates that his central missionary message concerns the event of Jesus' resurrection and, in particular, how this event proves him to be the true Lord of the world, exalted above all earthly masters and rulers.

But Romans 1:2–4 also has a striking parallel in 2 Timothy 2:8, another passage that, according to most scholars, relies on an early creedal formula. In this passage we hear the older apostle handing over the baton to his faithful co-worker Timothy, reminding him of his role, life, doctrine, and "gospel." The apostle writes: "Remember Jesus Christ, raised from the dead, descended from David. This is my gospel."

This is my gospel. It couldn't be any simpler. Paul's gospel is not so much focused on the doctrines of salvation but on the historic events of Jesus' messianic credentials—his resurrection from the dead and Davidic lineage. Note again that this summary corresponds precisely to the portrait of Jesus found in the Gospels of Matthew and Luke: beginning with Jesus' Davidic, kingly credentials and concluding with his vindicating resurrection. These two events (birth/resurrection) are like two bookends holding the story of Christ together.

Another of Paul's gospel presentations is found in 1 Corinthians 15:1–5, where he reminds the church of the message he first preached to them, and by which they were converted:

> Now, brothers, I want to remind you of the gospel I preached to you, which you received and on which you have taken your stand. By this gospel you are saved, if you hold firmly to the word I preached to you. Otherwise, you have believed in vain. For what I received I passed on to you as of first importance: that Christ died for our sins according to the Scriptures, that he was buried, that he was raised on the third day according to the Scriptures, and that he appeared to Peter, and then to the Twelve.

This paragraph reads like a plot summary of the passion narrative found in any one of the Gospels. Again, its emphasis is on events— Jesus' death, resurrection, and appearances. These events form the core of what Paul called the "gospel I preached to you." This is not to say that an interpretation of these events is not part of the gospel. Indeed, in the above formula, the historic event of Jesus' death is linked to the doctrine of sin and atonement. The point, however, is that theological significance is rooted in historic event, and in proclaiming the gospel, this is where it belongs. This passage also reveals Paul's emphasis on the death, resurrection, and appearances of Jesus as the core of the gospel. Interestingly, this emphasis is found in each of the Gospels as well. On average, an impressive 20 percent of the material in the Gospels focuses on the events of Jesus' death, resurrection, and appearances.

The importance of the above creedal statements should not be underestimated, for they are rare glimpses into the missionary proclamation of the first Christians, and of the Pauline missionaries in particular. In his letters, Paul (and the other apostles) had no reason to repeat their missionary preaching at great length. The gospel tends to be a shared assumption throughout the epistles, always in the background but rarely brought to the fore. Thus, the few hints we have about what was "first delivered" are of paramount importance to anyone interested in missional proclamation, or evangelism.

Another passage in which Paul explicitly articulates something of the gospel is Romans 2:16, where he writes: "This will take place on the day when God judges people's secrets through Jesus Christ, as my gospel declares." In this passage, Paul gives us one more piece of the gospel puzzle. Jesus' life does not end with his resurrection, appearances, and ascension into heaven. The story of Jesus reaches its climax when, as the Messiah, he returns to judge the world on God's behalf. This completes the story of Christ. This completes the gospel. This is the climactic demonstration of the universal reign of God through Christ.

The passages we have just looked at were all written to believers to remind them of the gospel Paul had preached to them. But in Acts 13 we have an example of Paul's evangelistic preaching, a presentation of the gospel aimed at unbelievers. It is so informative it is worth quoting a large portion of the passage:

After removing Saul, he made David their king. He testified concerning him: "I have found David son of Jesse a man after my own heart; he will do everything I want him to do." From this man's descendants God has brought to Israel the Savior Jesus, as he promised. Before the coming of Jesus, John preached repentance and baptism to all the people of Israel. As John was completing his work, he said: "Who do you think I am? I am not that one. No, but he is coming after me, whose sandals I am not worthy to untie." Brothers, children of Abraham, and you God-fearing Gentiles, it is to us that this message of salvation has been sent. The people of Jerusalem and their rulers did not recognize Jesus, yet in condemning him they fulfilled the words of the prophets that are read every Sabbath. Though they found no proper ground for a death sentence, they asked Pilate to have him executed. When they had carried out all that was written about him, they took him down from the tree and laid him in a tomb. But God raised him from the dead, and for many days he was seen by those who had traveled with him from Galilee to Jerusalem. They are now his witnesses to our people. We tell you the good news: What God promised our fathers he has fulfilled for us, their children, by raising up Jesus. (Acts 13:22–32)

"We tell you the good news," says Paul. This is his gospel presentation, anchored entirely in the Jesus event. The sermon concludes: "Therefore, my brothers, I want you to know that through Jesus the forgiveness of sins is proclaimed to you. Through him everyone who believes is justified from everything you could not be justified from by the law of Moses" (Acts 13:38–39).

Three things are particularly worth noting about this sermon. First, the focus of Paul's message is on the events of Jesus' life (it is a virtual summary of the Gospel narratives, particularly Mark and Luke). Second, the connection between the speech and the creedal summaries we looked at earlier in Romans 1 and 2 Timothy 2—with their emphasis on the Davidic, kingly rule of Jesus—is striking. Third, the passage contains an explicit reference to the Pauline doctrine of justification by faith and does so by rooting the doctrine firmly in the historic events of Jesus' Messianic rule, his life, death, and resurrection.

This brief study of Paul's use of the term "gospel" highlights his peculiar approach: he preaches the lordship and the resurrection of

Jesus as revealed in the events of his life, thus anchoring Christian proclamation in the story of Jesus, not the doctrines of the church. Indeed the doctrine of justification by faith flows out of a presentation of the Jesus event rather than the reverse. Evangelism is then much more about announcing the lordship of Jesus than the sinfulness of the unbeliever.

Evangelism as Inhabited Truth

This gels so nicely with what we saw earlier in Bosch's definition of mission as the alerting of people to the reign of God through Christ by both announcement and demonstration. If evangelism is the announcement piece, it makes sense that the message we announce relates to God proving his reign in the life, teaching, death and resurrection of Jesus. And so evangelism is proclamation, but it might not be preaching. We need to distinguish between these two approaches to communication. When not-yet-missional leaders refer to proclamation, they nearly always mean preaching. But the New Testament term *keryssein*, though often translated as "to preach," simply means the declaration of an event, a declaration that can be made both in word and deed. It refers to embodied truth, where the communicator's whole life inhabits the message being conveyed. Susan Hope, the canon of Sheffield, explains,

> The central conviction that Jesus is alive is woven into the heart and mind of the apostolic person: she is branded with it, marked with it; it is burned into the psyche. The message and the messenger becomes one.[14]

When we speak about the reign of God through Jesus, as revealed and confirmed in the events of Jesus' life and death, we do more than present a history lesson. Jesus is not simply an inspirational teacher. He is Lord.

I once overheard a conversation a Christian was having with his non-Christian friend. The non-Christian person asked something about his friend's lifestyle, and the Christian replied, "That's because I am inspired by the ancient teachings of Jesus." Now, there's technically nothing wrong with this answer. No doubt the young Christian's lifestyle is indeed shaped by the teachings of Jesus. And, who knows, maybe this was one of the first times he had introduced his faith into the conversation and he wanted to do so with sensitivity. My point isn't to suggest you ought never to use the phrase "the ancient teachings of Jesus" but simply to sound a caution about us only speaking of Jesus like some long-distant guru from whose ancient wisdom we draw for our lives. It's not unlike someone becoming obsessed with the writings of the Marxist revolutionary Leon Trotsky and quoting him at appropriate junctures in a conversation, claiming Trotsky's wisdom shapes their values and lifestyle (I know someone like this, actually). That's fine as far as it goes, but Leon Trotsky is not Lord. He does not rule the heavens and the earth. The uncomfortable nature of evangelism is that at some point (not necessarily *every* point) in a relationship, the supreme lordship of God through Christ must be announced. But remember, the lordship of Jesus must be an inhabited truth. His lordship in our lives ought to become apparent to our close friends and colleagues by our actions as well as our words. This is not an evangelistic technique. It is an obvious outcome of Jesus' lordship. As Stanley Hauerwas and William Willimon say, "The only way for the world to know that it is being redeemed is for the church to point to the Redeemer by being a redeemed people."[15]

This notion of evangelism as inhabited truth is not unique to general communication theory. In a world where advertisers, politicians, and snake-oil salesmen seem to be everywhere, vying desperately for our assent, the desire for a credible speaker of the truth is palpable. We desire true eloquence, the kind Ralph Waldo Emerson defined as "the art of speaking what you mean and are." He suggested that "the reason why anyone refuses his assent to your opinion, or aid to your benevolent design, is in you. He refuses to accept you as a bringer of truth, because, though you think you have it, he feels that you have it not. You have not given him the authentic sign."[16] Or as Sinclair Lewis's caustic character, evangelist Elmer Gantry, demonstrated, if you can fake authenticity, you've got it made. But seriously, evangelism is announcing the reign of God through Jesus, it is about recounting how the historic event of the incarnation, the crucifixion, and the resurrection attest to that reign, and it is about embodying that truth, stepping boldly into our task to be the "authentic sign" in our current day and age. If we claim that the gospel is concerned with the beautiful truth that heaven and earth have been drawn close by Jesus' death and resurrection and that God is putting everything right in this world, then such a truth must be communicated by a beautiful witness, an authentic sign that this rightness (or *shalom*) is embodied in our lives.

Balancing Announcement and Demonstration

And so we return to where we began, with the recognition that it is impossible to separate the announcement of God's reign from its demonstration. They are so intertwined it should be considered foolish even to try to unravel them. As David Bosch says, "There is in Jesus' ministry no tension between saving from sin and saving from physical ailments, between the spiritual and the social."[17] And neither should there be in our ministries today. Healing the sick, challenging unjust political and social structures, feeding the poor, embodying the values of the reign of God, telling others about the Jesus event—these are all examples of Emerson's "authentic sign." They are all facets of God's mission in this world, the mission of putting all things right. This is beautifully expressed by Lesslie Newbigin when he says,

> The salvation of which the gospel speaks and which is determinative of the nature and function of the church is—as the very word itself should teach us—a making whole, a healing . . . the restoration of the harmony between man and God, between man and nature for which all things were created.[18]

Our involvement with this restoration will include both our lips and our hands. It will involve evangelism, advocacy, peacemaking, worship, and proclamation as well as service, justice-seeking, healing, building, and feeding. Having abandoned any fears or concerns about which should be the priority, we are freed to respond to whichever need presents itself most apparently in any given situation. Where we encounter unbelief, we will announce the reign of God. Where we encounter poverty, we will demonstrate the reign of God. Since the reign of God covers all human experience, so should the mission of his people. Latin American evangelical leader René Padilla says,

Comprehensive mission springs from comprehensive salvation. Salvation is wholeness. Salvation is total humanization. Salvation is eternal life, life in the Kingdom, life that begins here and now and touches every aspect of man's being.[19]

Or as Susan Hope says, "The relationship . . . between mission and healing is a vital one. Healings—ecological, communal, individual—are signs of the kingdom. . . . Healings are what Roland Allen has called 'sermons in act,' words of the kingdom written in the stuff of biological and natural life."[20] When we ask ourselves what the implications of this might be in our churches, we need to look no further than our own backyard. The amazing success of the Korean American church can be put down to this very approach to intertwining announcement and demonstration. In his challenging book *The Next Evangelicalism*, Soong-Chan Rah observes,

The simple but true answer to what has spurred this phenomenal growth in the Korean American church is prayer and the work of God. At the same time, God's spiritual work often corresponds to a number of sociological factors that contribute to the growth of the church. God worked through various social factors to bring about revival in the Korean immigrant community.[21]

Subtitling his book *Freeing the Church from Western Cultural Captivity*, he makes the case that this predilection for separating and prioritizing either evangelism or social action has been a Western cultural construct. In the Korean American church, such a separation hasn't occurred, with startling results. While he identifies a number of characteristics that have contributed to the success of the Korean immigrant church—worship in the heart language of the immigrant, maintenance of homeland culture, the importance of community life—he sees the harmony between evangelism and social service as a key value:

The Korean immigrant church takes a holistic approach to evangelism. . . . The role of the church extends beyond simply gathering on Sunday to go through the rituals of a worship service. The Korean church provides for the primary cultural needs of displaced group. When the secondary systems of American society fail them, the Korean immigrants turn to the strong primary cultural systems available in the Korean church. Evangelism is not simply the employing of secondary systems that creates a program to be implemented; instead, evangelism is the engagement of life on all levels—serving a community in need and providing the services that demonstrate the kingdom of God to those who may be experiencing a sense of displacement in the kingdom of the world.[22]

Something similar is occurring among the urban poor in cities across the US. In Portland, Oregon, a wonderfully integrated example of evangelism and service is happening in Barberry Village. As quaint as it sounds, Barberry Village is in fact a thirty-six-year-old apartment complex in the heart of Rockwood, one of the toughest neighborhoods of Gresham, in the Portland area. Beset by the twin evils of poverty and crime, the residents of the 180 apartments of Barberry Village find life very challenging. About nine out of ten students at the two local elementary schools receive federally subsidized meals. Roughly 30 percent of the people who live in the area have no health insurance. Lawlessness is fueled by a MAX rail line that barrels through on East Burnside, just a half block from the apartment complex. Drug dealers and prostitutes often slip in and out of the neighborhood on the MAX, stealing past the no-trespassing sign at the entrance of the chain-link fence that surrounds Barberry Village. The only other people who visit the neighborhood as often are the police who receive daily call-outs to the area.

Several years ago, two young men in their early twenties, David Knepprath and Josh Guisinger, felt called by God to move into Barberry Village. Together with a couple of friends they rented a three-bedroom apartment in the complex. They put two sets of bunk beds in one room and used the other two bedrooms as an office and a closet. Their goal: create a sense of community in a chaotic neighborhood overrun with drugs, prostitution, and gangs.

Once inside the complex, they began a process of slowly but surely transforming the neighborhood. They handed out free cookies to their neighbors. They provided meals to those in need. They lobbied the management company to install more lighting and CCTV cameras to increase security. They encouraged the residents to attend, and later organize, community meals. They ran children's programs during school vacations. They helped residents move in or out. They've thrown birthday parties for neighbors. They cleaned up one woman's flooded apartment. In other words, they were just really good neighbors.

Police officers are still dispatched to Barberry Village on a regular basis, but the *Oregonian* recently reported that neighbors say the complex is safer, friendlier, and better for children. The paper even quoted a former manager calling Knepprath and Guisinger a "godsend." The article concluded,

> Many of their neighbors say Knepprath, Guisinger and the young men and women who followed them have made the complex a better place to live. Instead of staying holed up in their apartments, neighbors now go outside and get to know one another. They invite each other over for dinner. It's more like a neighborhood than an anonymous apartment complex.[23]

Having converted a terrifying apartment complex into a real neighborhood, they have catalyzed a sense of community in which conversation occurs, making it much more likely for evangelistic conversations to happen in organic, everyday ways.

Recently I worked with a major denomination to develop a series of missional indicators, the bare minimum requirements of a church daring to call itself missional or mission-shaped. It is by no means an exhaustive list, but it was an attempt to encourage churches—whether mega, house, simple, emerging—to strive for the kind of missional balance I have been discussing. We eschewed any reference to styles of worship or particular programs or ministries. We were looking for a broadly accessible matrix of missionality that a house church of 25 people or a megachurch of 2500 could adopt and expand upon. Beginning with a definition that "a mission-shaped church both announces and demonstrates the reign of God through Christ, both locally and globally, in the way of Jesus," we developed these indicators under three categories—announcement, demonstration, and the way of Jesus. I present them here as one denomination's attempt to inculcate genuine missionality among their network of churches:

1. A mission-shaped church *announces* the reign of God through Christ, locally and globally. This could be evidenced by

a. Regular opportunities for response to the gospel within the life and mission of the church;

b. Regular opportunities for members to hear of evangelistic projects and needs they might commit to;

c. A regular assessment of the needs of our immediate neighborhood/locality to determine whether certain ethnic, demographic, or subcultural groups are not hearing the announcement of the reign of God through Christ;

d. A corporate commitment to at least one local and one global evangelistic focus;

e. Active and prayerful consideration as to how we can be involved with planting a new congregation;

f. A commitment to regularly pray as a whole church for non-Christians to turn to Jesus, whether they be found locally or globally.

2. A mission-shaped church *demonstrates* the reign of God through Christ, locally and globally. This could be evidenced by

a. The fostering of a community life that models compassion, generosity, hospitality, and justice as expressions of the love of Jesus;

b. Regular opportunities for members to hear of effective community development projects and needs they might commit to;

c. A regular assessment of the needs of our immediate neighborhood/locality to determine whether certain ethnic, demographic, or subcultural groups are not benefiting from the demonstration of the lordship of Jesus;

d. A corporate commitment to at least one local and one global initiative aimed at addressing injustice, alleviating suffering, or showing practical love in Jesus' name;

e. An annual review of our budget and the degree to which our missional priorities are reflected in our financial commitments;

f. A commitment to regularly pray as a whole church for the needs of our world, locally, regionally, nationally, and globally.

3. A mission-shaped church embodies mission *in the way of Jesus*. This could be evidenced by

a. Regular teaching from the Gospels about the missional priorities, lifestyle, and message of Jesus, and the fostering of a faith community that reflects this;

b. Regular opportunities for members to discern their own missional vocation;

   c. Regular training and resourcing for members to be able to incarnationally develop friendships and share their faith in culturally and relationally effective ways;

   d. Active reliance on the empowering Spirit in the announcement and demonstration of Jesus' lordship;

   e. Regular assessment of the time commitments of pastoral staff and lay leaders to determine that too much of their time is not spent on "in-house" church activities and that they are freed to engage regularly with unchurched people;

   f. Regular teaching on the needs of our world and ways members can become actively involved.

It has been a generation since the conversation among evangelicals about the reintegration of evangelism and social action began. And yet I fear that there has not been enough evidence that the church is taking such a reintegration seriously. My concern is that while people keep affirming both evangelism and social justice, it is rare to find many examples of what such an integration looks like. We have strident voices calling us not to forget the importance of evangelistic preaching and the essential nature of the Word gifts described in Scripture. We have others, equally stridently, calling us to move into disadvantaged urban communities to live among and serve the poor. It is not unusual for us to hear Bible teachers and pastors making passionate calls for evangelism, while people like those working with international aid agencies are making equally passionate calls for global justice. And while each side now publicly affirms and encourages the call of the other, I think we need more than lip service from preachers that justice is important or from activists that evangelism is important.

If the integration of both proclamation and demonstration is essential for biblical mission, we need more examples that could show us what a truly holistic gospel looks like. I get inspired by John Piper's energy for apologetics and evangelism. And I am deeply moved by World Vision's Rich Stearns's passionate cry for justice for the oppressed people of the world. But I'd also like to see what integrated faith-sharing and justice-seeking looks like—whether it's in an Indian slum, a Western church, or the halls of Cambridge or Harvard.

3

A MARKET-SHAPED CHURCH

How Membership Has Trumped Mission

At its heart, the gospel is news about God's
action and his reign, not his institution.

—David Bosch

It's my educated guess that a great deal of the excesses of the traditional attractional church derive from the assumption that church membership is the chief goal of the mission of the church. If you truly believed that the *primary* task of the church is to increase its membership, it would seem reasonable to do anything to attract new members. This explains the various stunts and tactics used by churches to essentially bribe people to attend or to bribe existing members to bring newcomers.

Watching television in a hotel room in Houston recently, I saw an advertisement pitched at children, telling them that they will automatically receive a free gift if they come to the kids' program at the church, and if they bring their parents to the worship service, they will be entered in a drawing to win a new Wii or a PS3. This seems to me to be bribery of the basest kind—aiming at the self-interest of children to get to their parents. It's not unlike supermarkets placing racks of chocolate and candy at their checkouts to entice children to pester their parents to buy it.

One church in Corpus Christi went even further one Easter. They decided to go all out to attract new members by giving away flat-screen televisions, skateboards, Fender guitars, furniture, and fifteen cars—yes, *cars*—at their Resurrection Sunday services. And even those who didn't win the big prizes walked away with something. The church gave away 15,000 gift bags, each packed with about $300 worth of free goods and services. With all these prizes at stake, the church's leaders expected to more than double their normal weekly attendance—between 15,000 and 20,000 people—for that Sunday. One car was given away at each of the main campus services and one at each of the church's four satellite locations. At the main campus they had to cut a large space in the back of the chapel's stage for the cars to fit through during the services.[1]

Now, you can't fault the church's generosity. Promoted as a $1 million giveaway, the actual value was much higher (the 15,000 gift bags alone were worth $4.5 million if all the goods and services coupons were cashed in), and it was all paid for by donations from church members. But it's not just megachurches that pull these stunts. I've also heard of a small church in Ohio that gave away $500 to a lucky attendee of their Easter services.

What would motivate this kind of largesse? Surely, the only thing that could generate this outpouring of generosity is the belief that getting people to attend (and eventually join) the church is the chief end of Christian mission. I guess if I really believed this was the case, I might find myself justifying this kind of a ploy too. But we need to put church membership and the attendance of church worship services in its proper place, in the context of the missio Dei. Church attendance is not the *primary* goal of Christian mission. As David Bosch says, "At its heart, the gospel is news about God's action and his reign, not his institution."[2] As we've noted, mission is alerting people to God's reign through Christ and should not be limited or reduced to simply alerting people to the address of our church building and the times of our services.

This isn't to say there is anything inherently wrong with inviting people to gather with believers to observe Spirit-filled worship and the winsomeness of Christian fellowship. I believe that ultimately when someone acknowledges the reign of God through Christ, the end result will indeed be incorporation into the family of believers who have also come under that reign. My concern is that we should allow church membership to be the outcome of Christian mission, not its goal. If we make the alerting of people to God's rule the *primary* task, then church membership will be a *secondary* outcome. We need to learn to stop putting the cart before the horse. Whenever we assume church attendance is the chief end of mission, we will find ourselves reducing evangelism to recruitment and mission to salesmanship with all its attendant abuses.

Treating Others like Objects

Of course, those people we are trying to bribe to attend our services sense this a mile away. They are used to being treated like a "market," with every business under the sun trying to find ways to sell them their product. They are jaded and cynical. They don't believe those commercials that tell them fast-food outlets are genuinely concerned with their health. They don't believe the mining industry's campaign to convince them that there's such a thing as "clean coal." And they don't believe for one minute that the big supermarket chains are really the "fresh food people." So, why do we think they would believe that a church really cares for them simply because it gives away free stuff in return for their attendance?

The leaders at the Corpus Christi church just mentioned justified their spending spree as an expression of grace. They claimed that by giving prizes away they were mirroring God's grace in Jesus. Said the lead pastor, "We're going to give some stuff away and say, 'Imagine how great heaven is going to be if you feel that excited about a car.' It's completely free—all you have to do is receive him."[3] But were those prizes really completely free? They were available only to those who attended the Resurrection Sunday services and whose names were lucky enough to be pulled from the barrel. Sitting in church, clinging to your ticket, hoping like crazy that your name is called as the lucky winner—does this sound like the grace of God to you? How far from the message of Jesus have we strayed when we think this is acceptable? I don't mean to harp on about the Corpus Christi church specifically. It is simply one of the lowest points in this trend of bribing attendees, and it reveals to us the lengths to which churches will go to increase their membership, believing they are fulfilling the mission of God by so doing.

In the end I think people feel as though they are being treated like objects, like numbers being fed into the big business of church. When they do attend such churches, possibly dragged there by their children desperate to win a new PlayStation, they no doubt read in the church's newsletter the report of last week's attendance and the total figure of that Sunday's tithe. Printed every Sunday in church newsletters and bulletin sheets across the country, the attendance figures and the weekly giving figures are a stark reminder of our numerical value to the churches we attend.

I heard about a church in Southern California that gives away a brand new Harley-Davidson motorcycle to the member who brings the most guests to church in a given year. Imagine being invited to church by a friend only to discover that he or she did it to stay in the running to win the new bike. Surely you'd feel used, another notch in your friend's race to the finish line on December 31. When I raised this with the person who told me quite proudly about this church growth strategy, he was a little taken aback. He had never considered how someone might feel under those circumstances. And there's the problem. Too few people are thinking about the impression these stunts have on those outside the church.

We are treating people like a market, seeing them as clientele, not image-bearers of the living God. Evangelism professor at Boston University's School of Theology Bryan Stone reacts strongly against a not-yet-missional approach that is more concerned with "scalps"—with the recruiting of numbers to church attendance—than with the genuine announcement of God's reign through Jesus. He says,

Cruciformity rather than triumph, growth, and expansion will be among the primary marks of evangelism practiced well, and the virtuous evangelist will be identified not so much by her expertise as by her discipleship. The church's evangelistic effectiveness will have to be measured by the clarity, consistency, and inhabitability of its testimony rather than its toleration by a world where value is measured in terms of utility.[4]

To what degree have Christians bought into this worldview where value is measured by utility? As mentioned earlier, just read your church's newsletter. If it lists each week's attendance and the amount of giving and plots that against the annual average, you know something is awry. Stone is right when he says cruciformity— Christ-centered discipleship—must be a primary mark of effective evangelism. More on cruciformity later, but for now it is enough to make the point that when we aim at church attendance, all manner of abuses can occur. When we aim at making disciples as an expression of the reign of God through Jesus, things are different. It doesn't mean there won't be numerical growth, but it will be a by-product, not the goal. In this way, the gathered community of faith is focused on God and his reign, not on me and my needs. Is it any wonder churchgoers are so consumeristic in their approach to church? It's because we have treated them as such.

Consumer Christianity

My argument for making church membership a secondary outcome emerges from what I believe to be a biblical understanding of mission. But there are also practical reasons for embracing this reign-centered approach. If the institutional church is the only doorway to experiencing the reign of God, we are in an increasingly tenuous position as institutional religion loses its grip in society. Some years ago I met a businessman who, upon hearing that I write about the church's place in society, told me that the church's biggest problem is that it has a good product but that its "delivery system is screwed." For him, our "product" is Jesus, and he still has great currency and appeal in society today, but the delivery system—the church—no longer gets our product to our "market." Of course, he spoke in these terms precisely because he is not a churchgoer or a professing Christian. It irks me when church leaders speak about products and markets, but I understood why this businessman spoke this way. If he is right, and people are interested in Jesus but not inclined to attend church, then no wonder we end up having to bribe them with cash and cars to come to our services.[5]

And yet, even with all these ecclesial bells and whistles, churches struggle to hold on to their membership anyway. In 2006 Thom Rainer set off what the *New York Times* referred to as "the 4 percent panic attack" in his book, *The Bridger Generation*. He claimed to have conducted research that showed if current trends continue, only 4 percent of teenagers will be Bible-believing Christians as adults. That would be a sharp decline compared with 35 percent of the current generation of baby boomers, and before that, 65 percent of the World War II generation.[6]

While some critics say the statistics are greatly exaggerated, there was enough consensus among evangelical leaders that they risk losing their teenagers to prompt a forty-four-city leadership summit to discuss the matter. More than 6,000 pastors attended. One of the organizers, Ron Luce, founder of Teen Mania, was quoted as saying, "I'm looking at the data and we've become post-Christian America, like post-Christian Europe. We've been working as hard as we know how to work—everyone in youth ministry is working hard—but we're losing."[7]

That same year, the board of the National Association of Evangelicals, an umbrella group representing sixty denominations and dozens of ministries, passed a resolution deploring "the epidemic of young people leaving the evangelical church."

In 2008, the Pew Forum on Religion and Public Life found that 44 percent of Americans said they no longer adhered to the faith of their childhood. Compare that with the 1955 Gallup poll that showed that only 15 percent had switched their childhood religious affiliation.

It seems that when we make church attendance the goal and we try every inducement we can to get and keep people attending, it doesn't work in the long run. Treated like consumers by the church, young Christians are abandoning the church in the same way they abandon any other product with which they get tired. In the same way that they used to be into MySpace or Facebook or online gaming or clubbing but outgrew them, they used to be into church but outgrew that as well. They have been completely and utterly immersed in this form of consumptive Christianity, and we shouldn't be surprised when they toss the church aside like their old, outmoded iPod. In a *New York Times* piece, Jeffrey MacDonald concluded, "Americans now sample, dabble and move on when a religious leader fails to satisfy for any reason."[8]

But how are we to find our way out of this situation? As renowned biblical scholar Walter Brueggemann says, "The contemporary American church is so largely enculturated to the American ethos of consumerism that it has little power to believe or to act."[9] Addressing this topic in his book *The Divine Commodity*, Skye Jethani details the outcomes of consumptive religion in disturbing detail. Of consumerism in general he says,

> Consumerism has created a culture that values style over substance, image over reality, and perception over performance. . . . "Brands, not products!" became the rallying cry for a marketing renaissance led by a new breed of companies that saw themselves as "meaning brokers" instead of product producers. Successful companies discovered what philosopher Jean Baudrillard had known for decades: "Consumption is a system of meaning." We define our identity and construct meaning for our lives through the brands we consume.[10]

Jethani then refers to the titanic marketing brawl between Apple and Microsoft for the hearts and minds of consumers as the perfect example of this. And there is no better example of that struggle than the now well-known Apple commercials featuring a hip, relaxed young man, played by the popular actor Justin Long, who casually introduces himself to us with, "Hi, I'm a Mac." Next to him stands an awkward, pudgy, middle-aged guy in a suit, who stiffly responds, "I'm a PC." The message is loud and clear. Owning a Mac computer makes you cool. Apple sells identity, not just computers. So does Nike. And McDonald's. And so on. The danger arises when the church steps into this arena and assumes it must compete with all the other products vying for our allegiance. Then the church falls into the trap of promoting itself as a brand. Our T-shirts have to be cooler. Our music has to be hipper. Our product has to be sexier. And not long after that, it's easy for people to simply see their faith as a brand, a label, a basis for identifying with certain others and distinguishing oneself from others still. The end result, Jethani predicts, is immature Christians with a flimsy sense of identity and little real faith:

> In his column, Gordon MacDonald, a pastor for over forty years and author of dozens of books, pondered why our churches are filled with so many infant (immature) Christians. Given the abundance of resources available, why aren't there more mature men and women of God to emulate and celebrate? . . . MacDonald . . . wonders "what's been going wrong? Bad preaching? Shallow books? Too much emphasis on a problem-solving, self-help kind of faith?" Could it be that the consumer values—both inside and outside the church—which form the uncontested foundation of our preaching, books, and ministries are fundamentally designed to promote puerility and oppose maturity in all its forms?[11]

We raise our children in this consumptive Christian culture, no different from the consumer culture outside the church, and then we wonder why they leave the church in droves as soon as they get the chance. All we ever asked was allegiance to a brand, albeit the Christian brand. But just as one can change their image, their favorite brands, their music tastes, their style, their appearance, one can also change their religion if that religion means nothing more to them than any other old product. Nothing is precious. Everything has some utility. When I'm convinced that everything in the world has been designed to meet my needs in some way, I begin to believe those needs are the most important thing in the world. When we present the gospel merely as a utility, is it any wonder people no longer see its preciousness but look at it as a product for meeting our needs? Sarah Michelle Gellar, the star of the '90s cult classic television series *Buffy the Vampire Slayer*, epitomized consumptive religion perfectly when she said, "I consider myself a spiritual person. I believe in an idea of God, although it's my own personal ideal. I find most religions interesting, and I've been to every kind of denomination: Catholic, Christian, Jewish, Buddhist. I've taken bits from everything and customized it."[12]

Good for her. We Christians might look down our noses at this self-centered form of spirituality, but is the church really encouraging anything different? Don't many people in the church customize their religious faith as well, shaping it to suit their preferences and lifestyle? Is it possible that our favorite worship style is just another form of branding, of self-identification? For that matter, is the declaration of our favorite preacher another form of branding? I like Brian McLaren. I like Rob Bell. I like John Piper and Mark Driscoll. To me this often doesn't sound all that different from, Hi, I'm a Mac. And in the midst of all this, ministers and pastors are forced into having to work ever harder to satisfy the burgeoning needs of their congregations. In the *New York Times* op-ed piece referred to earlier, minister Jeffrey MacDonald bemoans this burden to meet the consumer needs of his congregation:

> In the early 2000s, the advisory committee of my small congregation in Massachusetts told me to keep my sermons to 10 minutes, tell funny stories and leave people feeling great about themselves. The unspoken message in such instructions is clear: give us comforting, amusing fare we want or we'll get our spiritual leadership from someone else.[13]

Where the missional conversation helps in this respect is that it eschews preferences for comfort, style, and denominational branding and invites us to look outward to where the missio Dei is at work among the poor, the marginalized, the lost, and the beleaguered. It demands of us the kind of selflessness and devotion to which Jesus called his first followers. MacDonald continues, speaking in the same vein:

> When they're being true to their calling, pastors urge Christians to do the hard work of reconciliation with one another before receiving communion. They lead people to share in the suffering of others, including people they would rather ignore, by experiencing tough circumstances—say, in a shelter, a prison or a nursing home—and seeking relief together with those in need. At their courageous best, clergy lead where people aren't asking to go, because that's how the range of issues that concern them expands, and how a holy community gets formed.[14]

Mere church attendance requires very little of us. And with the inducements being offered by many churches, it actually promises to give something *to* us, not require something *of* us. Alerting people to the reign of God through Christ ought not be reduced to church marketing. It is a costly, sacrificial service we do for the world around us. And as MacDonald points out, that's how a holy community gets formed. Unfortunately, in an unreflective attempt to grow churches and attract numbers, some pastors have been prepared to offer congregations what they want rather than leading them where they might not initially want to go. This belief in growth at any cost assumes that all growth is good and that the primary indicator of God's blessing is bigger and bigger congregations irrespective of the missional quality of those congregations. It simply mirrors the political and economic assumption about our economy that all growth—*any* growth—is always good. As Bryan Stone helpfully points out,

> While evangelism may be many things and while its practice may entail multiple logics, the central and foundational logic of evangelism is the logic of *martyria*, a logic of truthfulness, clarity, and incarnation, rather than the logic of production, accomplishment, or making.[15]

Stone's assessment is that for many churches their mission has been reduced to evangelism and that in turn has been reduced to attracting attendees. It is, as he says, the logic of production, which values size, power, and achievement. We speak of *building* churches, of *increasing* our influence, of *taking* back ground. But the true and central logic of the announcement of God's reign is found in a deeper desire for truthful speech, for clear and honest communication, for integrity and relationship.

What Would the Market Do?

It interests me to note that the church seems so slavishly aligned with the logic of production and the market that it is unable to assess the biblical legitimacy of that paradigm. Now, I'm no economist, but it would seem to me that a good deal of the theoretical underpinning of free market economics is opposed by the teaching of Jesus. For example, Jesus reveals God to be a distinctly relational being, whose priority is not economic growth, but right relationships between humanity and himself and between human beings. His injunction for us to love God and our neighbor indicates his clear priority for relational wealth over financial wealth. Furthermore, his explicit teaching on the seductive nature of wealth and greed and the difficulty for the rich of gaining access to the kingdom of God must be considered. And yet the market dictates that all growth is good, all the time. Where did the churches learn this? Not from Jesus. In fact, I have heard a stock analyst say that the market can always be trusted because it is driven by fear and greed, two qualities that orient the market to self-correct toward growth over the long term. How is putting your trust in fear and greed a reflection of the universal reign of God through Christ?

Michael Schluter, founder of Britain's Relationships Foundation, presents what he sees as five primary moral flaws in free market economics. They are worth looking at because they highlight the degree to which corporate capitalism is challenged by the reign of God through Christ. I don't reiterate them here as the final word on capitalism, only to highlight the fact that the Western church seems to be in cultural captivity to that paradigm. First, Schluter addresses capitalism's exclusively materialistic vision. Capitalism rests on the pursuit of business profit and personal gain. In other words, it promotes the idolizing of money. Schluter says, "People are regarded by companies as a resource, or as a cost in the profit and loss account, devoid of relational or environmental context. So capitalism constantly has to be restrained from destroying the social capital on which it depends for its future existence."[16]

Schluter claims that this focus on capital lends itself to the idolatry of wealth at a personal level, and the idolatry of economic growth at a corporate and national level. Shareholders pursue personal wealth with little knowledge of how it is generated, and senior management with scant regard for pay structures at lower levels of the company, while customers are persuaded by advertising to pursue self-gratification in its many forms. It's not hard to see the degree to which the Western church has unwittingly adopted this paradigm, assuming that all church growth, in terms of membership and finances, is always good, no matter the cost.

Corporate capitalism's second moral flaw, according to Michael Schluter, is that it offers reward without responsibility. In the parable of the talents, Jesus implies that gaining money through interest on a loan is reaping where you haven't sown. Lenders may accept some small risk, but they accept no responsibility for how or where the money is used. Debt finance generally results in relational distance rather than relational proximity, because the lender usually has no incentive to remain engaged with, or even in regular contact with, the borrower. Likewise, in the workings of large corporations, shareholders generally have little say in decision-making. Most investors provide share capital through a financial intermediary, such as a pension fund. Often they don't know or care in which companies they hold shares. Even the financial intermediaries generally do little to influence company policy. Perhaps, Schluter says, instead of the slogan "no taxation without representation," we should adopt "no reward without responsibility, no profit without participation." Surely this is a supremely missional framework for thinking of our involvement in the church, rather than the consumerist mentality that pervades so many churches. Indeed, such a view would rule out the worst aspects of rewarding attendees with free cars and prizes for their children.

Schluter says that corporate capitalism's third moral failing arises from the limited liability of shareholders, which allows debts to be left unpaid when the company becomes insolvent. Worse, the unpaid creditors are often employees, consumers, and smaller companies supplying goods and services. Because the downside risks of borrowing are capped, while the upside risks aren't, management has been willing to borrow huge sums relative to the company's share capital and thus expand companies at a frantic pace. In the finance sector, incentive schemes often reward risk-taking excessively on the upside with no downside penalties, reflecting the risk position of shareholders. Consequent mega-losses have to be financed by taxpayers to limit wider economic fallout.

Schluter's fourth charge against corporate capitalism is that it disconnects people from place. In the Old Testament, the jubilee laws required all rural property to be returned free to its original family owners every fiftieth year. It is debatable whether Israel ever exercised this law, but in theory it was designed to ensure long-term rootedness in a particular place for every extended family. A by-product was to ensure a measure of equity in the distribution of property, which ensured a broad distribution of political power. By contrast, capitalism regards land and property as assets without relational significance. This greater flexibility and mobility undoubtedly brings material benefits. But as extended family members move away from one another and communities become more transient, they can no longer fulfill welfare roles. Grandparents can no longer help look after grandchildren, and responsibility for care of older people and those with disabilities falls on the state, with the costs having to be met from tax revenues.

Schluter's final charge is that free market economics provides inadequate social safeguards. It has no concept of protecting the vulnerable through constraints on the market. Deregulation limits constraints on consumer credit, although the devastating consequences of debt for personal health and family relationships are well known.

Deregulation ensures labor is available for hire twenty-four hours a day, seven days a week, whereas biblical law protected a day a week for non-work priorities, including rest, worship, and family. The adverse consequences of these flaws start with family and community breakdown. Schluter says,

> The greater wealth of some sections of society in capitalist nations has to be set against the greater "relational poverty" which extends to an ever greater proportion of the population. The danger is that over time these relational problems become self-reinforcing and self-replicating.[17]

Another consequence of capitalism's failings over the longer term is a huge growth in government spending. As the number of damaged households increases, so does the size of the bureaucracy. Government spending on welfare has reached a level many regard as unsustainable, Schluter argues, yet without it many vulnerable people would have little or no physical or emotional support. As state agencies take over many of the roles of family and local community, they undermine the reasons why these institutions exist and thus further lower people's loyalty and commitment to them.

When filmmaker Oliver Stone wrote and directed the iconic 1989 film *Wall Street*, starring Michael Douglas as the corporate raider Gordon Gekko, he thought he was producing a scathing exposé of the greed and the hubris of the big end of town. Gekko was a cutthroat swashbuckler of a stockbroker who sneers "Lunch is for wimps," while allowing his unchecked workaholism and self-interest to amass his not inconsiderable fortune. His downfall at the end of the film was intended as a morality tale, revealing the hollowness and stupidity of the ambition-served-raw corporate atmosphere of the 1980s. But some audiences saw it differently. Corporate America loved *Wall Street*, with stock traders and company execs lining up to see it, guffawing loudly when Gekko famously declares, "Greed, for lack of a better word, is good. Greed is right, greed works. Greed clarifies, cuts through, and captures the essence of the evolutionary spirit. Greed, in all of its forms; greed for life, for money, for love, knowledge has marked the upward surge of mankind." Stone might have intended that piece of dialogue to be ironic, but it was quoted over and over as justifying the excesses of corporate capitalism.

My point here isn't to propose some anti-capitalistic political agenda. As I said, I am no economist, and it seems to me that all alternative economic visions are just as flawed but in different ways. My point, rather, is to suggest that the church's very understanding of its purpose and mission is often shaped more obviously by the free market than by the teaching of Jesus. Michael Schluter urges Christians to search urgently for a new economic order based on biblical revelation. I'll leave that discussion to the experts in that field, and in the meantime I'll continue to call the church to abandon consumer Christianity, with its highly materialistic vision, its desire for reward without responsibility, its disconnect from place, and the contribution it can make to social and family breakdown in the pursuit of its own growth.

Writing back in 1983, Lesslie Newbigin bemoaned the fact that "Christians believed it was impossible to interfere with the workings of 'economic laws,' that the writ of Christ's kingship did not rein in the autonomous kingdom of economics, and that the best one could do was to offer charity to the victims."[18] What we require today is a radical rethink about the degree to which our churches have unwittingly embraced what Bryan Stone calls the logic of production, and an uncoupling from that paradigm, setting churches free to embrace the alternative paradigm presented by Jesus, a paradigm of truthfulness, love, and incarnation. Or to quote Stone again, a logic of *martyria*.

The Logic of *Martyria*

The Greek word *martyria* refers usually to testimony given by witnesses, or a kind of legal deposition. In the New Testament it is invariably translated as "bear witness" and is applied to those who bear witness to the divine nature and origin of Jesus. When Bryan Stone speaks about us abandoning the logic of production and embracing the logic of *martyria*, he is in step with what we heard from David Bosch—namely, that the church's mission is to bear witness to the universal reign of God through Christ. But note the fact that the New Testament, particularly in John's Gospel, is explicit that this logic of witness was first modeled to us by the Triune God. Jesus bears witness to his own nature, as does his Father and the Spirit. Indeed, witness-bearing is a key expression of the relations between the persons of the Trinity.

In John 8, Jesus is challenged by the Pharisees who demand greater proof of his messianic identity than his own testimony, but Jesus retorts, "Even if I testify on my own behalf, my testimony is valid, for I know where I came from and where I am going. But you have no idea where I come from or where I am going" (John 8:14). Take that! But it's not only Jesus' words about himself that bear witness to his identity. His primary tool of *martyria* was of course his miracles, which were not just acts of kindness but witness-bearing works to his divine nature and origin. As Jesus says, "For the very work that the Father has given me to finish, and which I am doing, testifies that the Father has sent me" (John 5:36). And, "The miracles I do in my Father's name speak for me" (John 10:25).

This is nowhere more obvious than when the imprisoned John the Baptist sends emissaries to seek out Jesus for a confirmation that he is indeed the Messiah they were expecting. Moved to affirm his cousin's faith in him, Jesus demonstrates his credentials in the most powerful way he can: "Go back and report to John what you have seen and heard: The blind receive sight, the lame walk, those who have leprosy are cured, the deaf hear, the dead are raised, and the good news is preached to the poor" (Luke 7:22).

While Jesus' words and works testify to his own identity, so the Father also embraces this witness-bearing work. John reports Jesus as saying, "I am one who testifies for myself; my other witness is the Father, who sent me" (John 8:18). And later in his first epistle, John is forthright in his belief in the Father's witness to his Son: "Anyone who believes in the Son of God has this testimony in his heart. Anyone who does not believe God has made him out to be a liar, because he has not believed the testimony God has given about his Son" (1 John 5:10).

And of course, John also features the role of the Holy Spirit in witness-bearing on behalf of Jesus when he recounts Jesus' words to the disciples: "When the Counselor comes, whom I will send to you from the Father, the Spirit of truth who goes out from the Father, he will testify about me" (John 15:26).

Since witness-bearing is so central to the persons of the Trinity, then by association the followers of the Triune God should see the logic of *martyria* as central to their life together. And what is the logic of witness-bearing? According to Bryan Stone, as quoted earlier, it is truthfulness, clarity, and incarnation. The church must recommit itself to the radical and alternative values of the kingdom and express truthful, clear witness-bearing in the form of incarnational mission. This obviously implies a decoupling of the church from the logic of the market and a rediscovery of what mission looks like when it's not shaped by big business.

In his book *The Great Giveaway: Reclaiming the Mission of the Church from Big Business*, David Fitch dreams of what a church might look like that steps out of the paradigm set for it by rampant capitalism. This is a paradigm, Fitch says, that has led evangelicals to individualize, commodify, and package Christianity and to turn their churches into capitalist businesses with CEO-style pastors judging success by the number of "decisions for Christ" produced. He challenges evangelical churches to think smaller (in terms of congregation size), place less focus on coercive evangelism, return to communal catechesis, offer more liturgical worship, and provide opportunities for small group intimacy where Christians can confess their sins, repent, read Scripture, and pray together regularly. Indeed, in his closing chapter he sketches the shape of a biblical church for the twenty-first century.[19] It is so beautifully idealistic and naïve that it made my heart sing. It is a church anchored around the logic of martyria, and I summarize his vision in the following points:

- Congregations will become smaller not bigger, but there will be more of them, many more, all teeming with life and joy and fresh hope;
- Congregations will be more racially and economically diverse;
- These congregations will be known for their servanthood in their neighborhoods by practicing hospitality, and welcoming strangers into their homes;
- Christians will evangelistically invite strangers to the gospel;
- Congregations will openly and graciously share life's joys and sufferings with each other and the sharing of meals will be central to their life together;
- Congregations will value children and emphasize the importance of raising children in the faith as an intrinsic part of the whole congregation;
- These congregations will be led by humble men and women who will listen attentively and suffer alongside their members;
- Congregations will develop a form of liturgy that shapes and strengthens disciples;
- Congregations will model what true community looks like for a new body politic for our age;
- There will be the renewal of monastic practices—confession, repentance, Bible reading, prayer—as these practices will strengthen the capacity and resolve for genuinely missional engagement.[20]

In 1969, a year after the tumultuous social upheaval of the 1968 student protests in Paris and Berlin, Belgrade and Prague, at a time when the church in Europe was struggling to deal with monumental social change, an idealistic young German priest was interviewed about the place of the church in modern society. He predicted the emergence of a leaner, more organic, less institutional church:

> From today's crisis, a church will emerge tomorrow that will have lost a great deal . . . She will be small and, to a large extent, will have to start from the beginning. She will no longer be able to fill many of the buildings created in her period of great splendor. Because of the smaller number of her followers, she will lose many of her privileges in society. Contrary to what has happened until now, she will

present herself much more as a community of volunteers . . . As a small community, she will demand much more from the initiative of each of her members and she will certainly acknowledge new forms of ministry and will raise up to the priesthood proven Christians who have other jobs . . . It will make her poor and a church of the little people . . . All this will require time. The process will be slow and painful.[21]

That German priest was Joseph Ratzinger, who ascended to the papacy in 2005 as Pope Benedict XVI. Forty years ago he dreamed of a humble church that no longer relied on its power, prestige, privilege, or finances, a church comprised of missional volunteers who developed new incarnational ministries and who took the mission of God to the poor and to "the little people" as empty-handed ones, filled only with the grace of God and the power of the Holy Spirit. Today, he presides over the biggest religious business in the world. Will a new generation of missional Christians be able to emerge and rediscover church and mission beyond the marketing paradigm that seemed to obsess their parents and their pastors? Will we be able to reclaim the mission of the church from big business? Will we be able to perceive of the mission of God as greater than the attraction of more consumptive Christians to our weekly public meetings and unleash a missional movement across the world, for the glory of the God who reigns universally through Christ? As renowned theologian Howard Snyder asserts,

> Kingdom people seek first the Kingdom of God and its justice; church people often put the church work above concerns of justice, mercy and truth. Church people think about how to get people into the church; Kingdom people think about how to get the church into the world. Church people worry that the world might change the church; Kingdom people work to see the church change the world.[22]

4

TRIUMPHANT HUMILIATION

The Cross as a Missional Paradigm for Holiness

His [Jesus'] was a wild holiness that calls to account all who refuse to deal with God, preferring instead to follow the lame dictates of a religion of ethical codes and pious rituals.

—Alan and Debra Hirsch

The following story appeared in *The Onion*, a publication well known for its biting satire on any and all subjects. This parody, titled "Heckled Christian Rock Band Knows How Jesus Felt," graciously allows us to examine an insidious form of pietism without using a true-life (and potentially humiliating) example. The quotes attributed to the band members are unfortunately not as far-fetched as we'd like to think they are.

When the Christian rock band Enter the Kingdom accepted a Friday night gig at rowdy Pat's Tavern in Columbia, Missouri, they ought to have seen things weren't going to end well for them that night. The four-piece band, all of whom met in a Bible study group, played a forty-five-minute set which included such songs as "Light of the Lord," "The Exalted," and "Glorious Salvation."

Soon after the band took to the stage, the patrons of Pat's Tavern made it evident that Christian rock was not their first choice in entertainment. Lead singer Andrew Walker certainly got the message: "Especially when the crowd started chucking food at our heads, that definitely hit it home."[1] But Enter the Kingdom played on bravely in the face of a tirade of obscenity hurled at them from every quarter. Even security joined in and heckled the band.

What is particularly interesting for our purposes are the responses the writer penned for the members of Enter the Kingdom—intended as satire but all too close to reality. Rather than concluding that either (a) Pat's Tavern wasn't the ideal venue for them, or (b) they weren't a very good band, they tried sanctifying what might have simply been an embarrassing night on stage. Indeed, they interpreted the dreadful night at Pat's Tavern as a Christlike experience.

Singer Andrew Walker summed it up this way: "We were always taught that Christ suffered for the sins of man, but it wasn't until our gig at Pat's Tavern that we actually understood what that meant. The fact that Jesus wasn't very popular in his day, or that people hated him for spreading a different kind of message, or even just the ridicule and humiliation he was forced to endure—it all became clear to us Friday night."

Bass player Kevin Clark compared the harrowing show to "what Jesus must have braved" at the hands of Pontius Pilate, claiming that while performing he also faced a series of false accusations, including being called nasty names by the crowd. "It was like the story of Jesus, unfolding right up there on that stage," he said. "And just like Christ, we did not retaliate for their cruel actions. Not even when the whole 'get off the stage' thing really got going."

This desire to legitimize their embarrassment reached its high point with the following comment by the band's guitarist, Bradley

Baldwin: "They were jealous and punishing us for our righteousness, because they couldn't face the power and truth of our songs."

I think it is reasonable to assume that the majority of patrons who frequent an establishment such as the fictitious Pat's Tavern would be the run-of-the-mill bar crowd. Their tastes in music might range from jazz to country to rock but would likely not include inspirational contemporary Christian music. And then there's the matter of musical aptitude—was this a good band or your basic garage band?

Why wouldn't the band consider the possibility that their songs were just not what the audience wanted that night? Why does the behavior of the bar patrons have to be explained as persecution, when it might simply be a high-spirited reaction to a bad rock band?

Let's move this into real-life application. I appreciate that humiliation is so horrifying an experience that justifying it in this way seems to be the only means for coping with it. To humiliate someone, even if it is just heckling an inappropriately booked band at your local tavern, is to tear at their soul, to devalue them, to dominate them. What gets me is the type of Christian perspective that has to spiritualize everything, to oversacralize every moment, and heighten every experience to that of life and death. It is a form of piety that assumes the perpetual innocence of the believer and the never-ending suspicion of unbelievers. It derives from a form of spirituality that, to quote Alan and Debra Hirsch, prefers "the lame dictates of a religion of ethical codes and pious rituals."[2]

The Lame Dictates of Pious Rituals

Maybe the patrons at Pat's Tavern in Columbia, Missouri, just thought Enter the Kingdom stunk. Maybe when your neighbor ignores you, it's not because he hates the light of the Lord that shines from you. Maybe he just thinks you're a jerk. Maybe we get most of the rejection we do because, well, we deserve it. It's no different from President George W. Bush explaining the September 11 terrorist attacks on New York and Washington as acts of violence perpetrated by people who hate us because of our freedom. While America was innocent that day and those acts of terror were perpetrated by violent and hate-filled men, the explanation that all Islamic extremists hate America because of her democratic freedom is a pietistic way of dodging the real issues. The worst forms of pietism make a person impervious to humility, unable to learn from an enemy or an outsider. Sadly, within many churches discipleship is often reduced to such pietism, and very often it's the worst form of pietism that demonizes outsiders and encourages a bunker mentality.

I believe there is a great difference between true godliness and this kind of self-serving pietism, which insists on withdrawal from anyone who doesn't share the same views on life as us. This kind of pietism really is a lie about the nature of true godliness, which is shown to us by Jesus as being more to do with engagement with brokenness than withdrawal from it. So what's wrong with pietism and how in particular does it lead us away from being missional? Essentially, pietism is about self-improvement. It is a resolute devotion to increased "holiness," a never-ending process of putting away sin and becoming more and more pleasing to God. This sounds good, but the view of God often taken by pietists is that of a far-off deity, removed from the sinfulness of human society, disgusted by the foibles and conceits of human nature. This is a form of religiosity that lifts itself aloft (though admittedly that may not be very far off the ground), separating itself from everyday life and contact with so-called sinners, whom one always refers to in the third person as though we ourselves are not sinners as well. In an effort to do this, pietists find themselves turning inward away from the world, in search of greater and deeper improvement. So it is the erection of a false standard of holiness, one that is generally sentimental, smarmy, and resentful, and which is then applied to the church by its dogmatic enthusiasts. It makes the pietist always right, always righteous, or more insidiously, always the victim. Any dissent, any disagreement, is seen as persecution. Such false pietism wants us to believe that they, the pietists, have a monopoly on righteousness, and that everyone else has a gross deficiency of it.

The problem with this is that it grants too much to the pietists. Their problem is not too much righteousness, but rather that they are *unrighteous*. Jesus said that we would not see the kingdom unless our righteousness *surpassed* that of the Pharisees. Pietism is condemned by its own profession—it leads directly to impiety and all manner of ungodliness. This is the tragically corrupt center of pietism. Pietistic homes may have rejected all kinds of things—cards, movies, slang, spicy foods, fiction, and all the rest of it—but these same homes can be filled with anger, self-importance, lust, and abuse. Pietism is a whitewashed tomb, or as nineteenth-century German philosopher F. T. Vischer once quite colorfully put it:

> I have called pietism a scab, a suppuration of the best juices of the spirit. . . . The madness of pietism lies in the peculiarity of its interest in religion. . . . The pietist is religious as if religion is his trade, the pietist is he who goes around professing his religion, the pietist is the man who smells for religion. . . . A pietist must be a hypocrite.

I was once taken to task by someone who claimed it was better to be a pietist (like him) than a cynic (presumably, he thought, like me). Aside from defending myself from the charge of cynicism, I replied that I thought at least humility is on the cynic's side. After all, the cynic can be cynical about his cynicism, while the pietist can never seem to be cynical about his pietism.

But as I mentioned earlier, the pietistic tradition is killing the church's missional orientation. It turns the church in on itself. It judges newcomers. It insists on exacting and unrealistic standards. And it can play the judge and executioner with chilling relish.

I'm inclined to think the two primary motivators for this kind of internally oriented and highly judgmental spirituality are laziness and fear. Pietism is lazy because it outsources the need to do the daily work of keeping in step with the Spirit of God. Discerning what Jesus would do in any given situation, especially when we live our lives among those who don't share our faith, or among the poor and the marginalized, is actually hard work. It's not a set-and-forget kind of spirituality. You need to be prepared to keep on your toes, stay alert to the Spirit and attentive to those to whom God has sent you. Pietism is easy in one respect. You don't have to do the difficult, focused work of seeking God's will in any given situation. You simply have to follow the externally determined set of rules of pietism. Letting pietistic conventions guide you takes all the elbow grease out of our spirituality. Don't drink, don't smoke, don't gamble, and don't hang out with people who do. But when we engage incarnationally in our neighborhood, we will be required to make multiple little (and some big) judgment calls every day. It requires godly verve, flexibility, and energy to be missional.

On the other hand, I think pietism is a fear-based version of Christianity. And this fear runs in two different directions. First, pietists are afraid of disappointing or offending God because they're not righteous enough. Well, they're never righteous enough. I have a friend who grew up in a fundamentalist Christian home, who as a little girl had rehearsed saying "Please forgive me for my sins" as quickly as she could, so when Jesus returned she could get it out just in time to cover any of the sins she'd committed since she'd last asked for forgiveness, lest she be dragged straight to hell. But second, pietists are afraid of everyone around them. They think all the non-Christians (and the liberal Christians) are out to get them, that everyone is laughing at them because of their faith, persecuting them because of their holiness. Both these types of fear paralyze pietists and stop them from moving into their world, making friends with their neighbors, or connecting with the lost and the poor. Fear, coupled with laziness, kills missional involvement stone cold.

The Square Halo

Wandering through the Vatican Museum in Rome once, I came across a beautiful mosaic fragment from the early eighth century. It depicts a reflective-looking Pope John VII holding a model of the oratory, or chapel, he built inside Old St. Peter's Cathedral. I hope the chapel ended up being more impressive than the model he is holding, because it looks rather like a small dog kennel—not what he had in mind, I'm sure. What impressed me about this picture, though, is that framing his slightly inclined head is a simple black square. When I enquired of my guide about this addition to an otherwise straightforward mosaic portrait, I was told that the black square was in fact John's halo. Taken aback, I told him I thought all halos were meant to be circular and glowing. Aren't they always beaming discs of godliness? My guide informed me that, in religious art, circular halos are reserved exclusively for Jesus, Mary, and for the saints. Occasionally God the Father is given a triangular halo to depict the Trinity, and the cardinal virtues—Faith, Hope, Charity, Prudence,

Temperance, etc.—were often given hexagonal halos. But the use of the square halo, though rare, was intended to depict a holy person who had not yet been canonized as a saint. Clearly Pope John VII was a good and respectable churchman, but at the time the mosaic was created he had not yet died and qualified for canonization.

Circular halos are intended to reflect the perfection of heaven, while the square halo reminds us that its bearer is still very much of the earth. I like the idea of my portrait being painted with me wearing a square halo, admittedly somewhat askew. It speaks of an earthy kind of spirituality, a down-to-earth holiness. I'm certainly no candidate for sainthood, but I have come face-to-face with Jesus, and I have, thanks to the gift of faith, committed myself to serving him and participating in the ongoing unfurling of his reign. The more I look to Jesus, the more I see him as the bearer of a square halo as well, albeit not askew like mine. His holiness is revealed through his everyday mercy and his goodness toward the poor and marginalized, not by his being above or beyond contact with sinners. If we want to emulate the righteousness of Jesus, we need to rediscover that his is a holiness revealed by contact with the broken things of this world, not by withdrawal from them. As N. T. Wright so marvelously puts it, referring to John's Gospel,

> [John] invites us to be still and know; to look again into the human face of Jesus of Nazareth, until the awesome knowledge comes over us, wave upon terrifying wave, that we are looking into the human face of the living God. And he leads us on, with our awe and bewilderment reaching its height, to the point where we realize that the face is most recognizable when it wears the crown of thorns. When John says "We beheld his glory," he is thinking supremely of the cross. And those who see this glory in this cross are, very shortly afterwards, commissioned to follow the one who has made his glory visible.[3]

This is a subject I dealt with in far greater detail in my previous book, with Alan Hirsch, *ReJesus*, in which we challenged our readers to rediscover the biblical face of Jesus and recognize the need to model our missional lifestyle on his. The cross therefore is not only the means by which our sins are forgiven, but it becomes the template for all subsequent Christian living. God's greatness is not sullied or diminished by his engagement with sinners, but crystallized through it.

You might recall the so-called Muhammad cartoons controversy in 2005, where twelve editorial cartoons, most of which depicted the Islamic prophet Muhammad, were published in the Danish newspaper *Jyllands-Posten*. This was done in an attempt to contribute to the debate regarding criticism of Islam and self-censorship. Rather than stimulating debate, it set off an explosive worldwide reaction by the Muslim community. This included setting fire to the Danish embassies in Syria, Lebanon, and Iran, storming European buildings, and desecrating the Danish flag in Gaza City. Why were these cartoons considered so insulting by some Muslims? Of course, there is a general prohibition within Islam on images of Muhammad. But to add to the insult, one cartoon portrayed the Prophet wearing a turban shaped as a bomb with a burning fuse, reinforcing the caricature of Muslims as terrorists for Muhammad. That being acknowledged, I mentioned to an Islamic leader at the time that it seemed like an extreme reaction to be storming and burning buildings over a few silly cartoons. He told me that he thought I, of all people, would understand their response. "After all," he said, "imagine how offended you would be if someone humiliated Jesus."

Humiliated Jesus? Surely the humiliation of Jesus is at the center of the Gospel story. Indeed, as N. T. Wright said earlier, the humiliation of Jesus is considered to be his crowning glory. The God of Jesus reveals his holiness not by the avoidance of humiliation but by embracing it. This is the opposite of pietism (either the Christian or Muslim versions) where one's holiness is revealed via separation. Cross-shaped holiness is the kind of godliness that is distilled and intensified by engagement, suffering, service, and sacrifice.

Cruciformity as a Missional Paradigm for Holiness

Whereas the term *cruciform* used to exclusively describe items shaped like a cross (the floor plan of a church, the arrangement of leaf blades and petals on a flower, the ligaments in the human body), in recent years a growing number of Christian leaders have begun using it and the related term *cruciformity* in respect to Jesus' nature and to our likeness to him. Indeed, it can be demonstrated that it was central to the apostle Paul's theology and ethics. This centrality was influenced by two main factors: (1) the revelation from the risen Christ to Paul regarding the centrality of the cross,[4] and (2) the common use of crucifixion by the Romans for criminals, including Christians.[5] As a result, when Paul writes about "the cross," he is referring to the crude implement used by the Romans to torture people to death, including Jesus, but he is also referring to something more than that—the very shape of Christian holiness and discipleship.

Cruciformity then can describe one's commitment to become more like Jesus. It is the shape of Jesus' incarnation of the nature of God and also therefore the shape that Jesus creates for every aspect of Christian discipleship. Wheaton College professor Jeffrey Greenman puts it this way:

> The cross is the paradigm for a disciple's life in the world. "If anyone would come after me, he must deny himself and take up his cross daily and follow me" (Luke 9:23). Taking up the cross means intentionally conforming our lives to the pattern of life shown in Jesus' death on the cross. . . . It is living by the "law of Christ," which means having a "ministry shaped by Christ's paradigmatic status-denying, other-regarding love."[6]

Throughout the New Testament, and particularly in Paul's letters, Christian discipleship is cross-shaped. As disciples, we follow a leader whose own path of obedience to God led him to the cross, a leader whose identity is revealed unmistakably by his wounds. We are a people whose identity is found in the crucified Jesus—not in our own strength. For this reason, the revelation of God in Christ, the shaping of Christian spirituality via Jesus' example, means that we see ourselves through this lens. Greenman continues,

> The cross is the supreme revelation of God's power-in-weakness, and the resulting paradox is that God's power is "made perfect in our weakness" (2 Cor. 12:9) just as God's power was made perfect in the self-emptying weakness of Jesus at the cross. . . . Christian leaders are people who live the Cross—humbling themselves; voluntarily divesting themselves of their rights and privileges; trusting not in their own wisdom; insisting not on their own way; doing nothing out of selfish ambition; seeking not their own advantage but the

benefit of others; in humility, considering others better than themselves; giving up their lives for the sake of the lost, the vulnerable, and the neglected.[7]

In other words, the cross and all it stands for counters the nullifying effects of the fear and laziness of which I spoke earlier. I can't emphasize this too strongly. When we adopt a cruciform spirituality, we are necessarily drawn outward, toward "sinners," not away from them. The cross is the supreme act of engagement. It is God's way of entering into the sin and brokenness of this world to redeem it and make friends with sinful people. Therefore, a spirituality based on cruciform principles is the very opposite of the frightened, lazy version modeled by pietism. Furthermore, the incarnation of Jesus shapes a robust spirituality that dares to accept that true godliness doesn't mean complete withdrawal from society. Jesus manages to be sinless and still grow up in Nazareth. He manages to be holy and still eat and drink with sinners, tax collectors, and prostitutes. He manages to be glorified while hanging naked and bloodied on the cross. His passion is the antithesis of fear and laziness. It is the ultimate in courage and work. And he calls his followers to a similar cross-shaped courage and work.

The Cross as Metaphor

References to the cross in the New Testament speak of it as being more than an instrument of torture; rather, it is a metaphor for that set of attitudes and actions expressed in and through Jesus that also define and describe the new life that a Christian disciple is called to pursue. The cross in effect became a symbol of the necessity of full commitment (even to the point of death) for those who would be Jesus' disciples. It was also a metaphoric symbol of Jesus' love and the thankful disciple's unreserved commitment to Jesus' lordship. This is obvious in Jesus' words to his disciples, "If anyone would come after me, he must deny himself and take up his cross and follow me. For whoever wants to save his life will lose it, but whoever loses his life for me will find it" (Matt. 16:24–25). The taking up of one's cross is a metaphor for full devotion. But note that this devotion, while seeming to court death, in fact brings life. This idea is echoed in John's Gospel, where Jesus, preparing for his own death, tells his disciples, "The hour has come for the Son of Man to be glorified. I tell you the truth, unless a kernel of wheat falls to the ground and dies, it remains only a single seed. But if it dies, it produces many seeds. The man who loves his life will lose it, while the man who hates his life in this world will keep it for eternal life" (John 12:23–25).

Often interpreted only as Jesus' promise of eternal life, these passages should be read as triumphant, exultant declarations of life—full life—in the here and now as well as for eternity. We must die to the false belief that we are the rulers of our own destiny and come alive to God's reign. When we do that, having handed the rule of our life to God, we become regenerative people, bearing fruit in the lives of others. Cruciformity involves such death, rebirth, and regeneration. *Vine's Expository Dictionary* says, "Crucifixion is metaphorically used of the renunciation of the world that characterizes the true Christian life."[8] But crucifixion is also metaphorically used to denote the embracing of the life offered under God's reign.

The Cross as a Paradigm

The cross is more than a metaphor or a symbol of Christian discipleship; it is a paradigm by which we can view Jesus as our example for life. When we speak about Jesus being the exemplar of missional living, we must not ignore the cross-shaped nature of that example. The apostle Peter illustrates this when he says, "To this you were called, because Christ suffered for you, leaving you an example, that you should follow in his steps" (1 Pet. 2:21). He goes on to address the specific implications of this for the suffering churches of Asia Minor—the avoidance of deceit, the refusal to retaliate, the submission to authorities, and so forth. Jesus' cross-shaped death, then, fashions a cross-shaped paradigm for seeing the outworkings of a life patterned on him. In reflecting on this passage in 1 Peter, John MacArthur says,

> In his death Jesus taught us how to live. We often look at his dying moments and observe that his death illustrates the seriousness of sin and the need for a savior to pay the price for our iniquity. We recognize that by his substitutionary death, he died in our place. But Peter said

that there's even more to the cross than that. Christ died not only for us, but also as an example to us. He died to show us how to live.[9]

This paradigm is not unique to Peter. It marinates the writings of Paul, who sees the suffering of Jesus not only as the means of righteousness with God but as a framework for all Christian service and life. In 1 Corinthians 4:12–16, he echoes Peter's words about enduring persecution or suffering as Jesus did, drawing on the cross as the paradigm for dealing with the curses and slander of others. But Paul also draws a cruciform paradigm for addressing all kinds of issues. In Romans, when addressing the ethical matter of dietary restrictions, Paul does so from a cross-shaped paradigm: "We who are strong ought to bear with the failings of the weak and not to please ourselves. Each of us should please his neighbor for his good, to build him up. For even Christ did not please himself but, as it is written: 'The insults of those who insult you have fallen on me'" (Rom. 15:1–3). In other words, when trying to think through what we can eat and when and with whom, think of it in cross-shaped terms. Ask yourself, In what ways does the example of Jesus contribute to my understanding of how to deal with this issue? Likewise, in the matter of the conduct of marital relations in the new community, Paul says, "Husbands, love your wives, just as Christ loved the church and gave himself up for her" (Eph. 5:25). Again, what might seem to be a personal and very private matter is addressed in completely cruciform terms. It's not as simple as asking what would Jesus do. It goes further: In what ways does the crucifixion create a template for me to be a better husband?

But remember, this doesn't take us back to the slavish devotion to legalism and fear that we see in the pietists. It's not suffering for suffering's sake. Paul celebrates this cruciform approach to living to the full when he says, "I want to know Christ and the power of his resurrection and the fellowship of sharing in his sufferings, becoming like him in his death" (Phil. 3:10). It is a death to self, but it is an embracing of his resurrected reign over my life. I should be free from fear and laziness, filled with his courage and his work, and the application of this work and this courage is to be made in all situations, whether in the face of persecution, in the thorny issue of food laws, or in the lifelong commitment to marriage.

Cruciformity as Missional Discipleship

How is this different from the poor old members of Enter the Kingdom, who clearly saw their bad night at Pat's Tavern as mirroring Jesus' persecution in Jerusalem? Weren't they seeing that night through a cruciform lens? Well, yes and no. Yes, they were thinking that their suffering mirrored that of Jesus and they drew some encouragement from that belief. But were they really suffering in the same way that Jesus did? If I do a bad job at my work and my supervisor reprimands me for it, is this cruciform suffering? If I suffer in some form as a result of my poor choices, am I suffering like Jesus? Or am I using Jesus as a salve to my bruised ego because I actually deserved that reprimand or the rejection of those people I offended? Sometimes our suffering or embarrassment is our own fault and shouldn't be attributed to the fact that everyone hates us because we're Christians. And sometimes, as in the case of that fateful night at Pat's Tavern, our witness to the reign of God through Christ is just off the mark and maybe we deserve the reaction we get. Genuine cruciform suffering is life-giving. Like Jesus, our decision to serve and love can be costly because there are forces at work in our world that prefer fear and laziness and death. But ultimately our suffering if it is truly cruciform should do what Jesus' suffering does—it should bring life. As John Piper, author of *Desiring God*, points out,

> Our suffering becomes an extension and presentation of Christ's suffering for those for whom he died. Suffering is not an accidental result of obedience. It is an ordained means of penetrating the peoples and the hearts of the lost.[10]

In Chapter 1, I mentioned the extraordinary work of Cambodian pastor Abraham Hang, working among evicted squatters in Andong, a resettlement slum outside Phnom Penh. His work is a brilliant balance of both the announcement and the demonstration of the reign of God through Christ, including the establishment of medical clinics, schools, better housing, a church, and transportation for workers to and from the city. His is a life-giving, thoroughly cruciform work. But he has also suffered. Indeed, moving his pregnant wife and child into a slum is suffering enough, but Abraham has also been harassed, threatened, and attacked by corrupt and cruel forces wanting him to abandon the community at Andong. The last time I saw him, Abraham had scabs and sores down his arm and leg from when he was pushed off his motorbike by thugs. His life is in danger because his life *brings life* in the midst of darkness. We see something similar in the lives (and deaths) of Dietrich Bonhoeffer, Simone Weil, and Martin Luther King. Their suffering penetrated the hearts of their enemies and the lost. And it makes sense of the words of Paul to the Corinthians when he wrote,

> We always carry around in our body the death of Jesus, so that the life of Jesus may also be revealed in our body. For we who are alive are always being given over to death for Jesus' sake, so that his life may be revealed in our mortal body. So then, death is at work in us, but life is at work in you. (2 Cor. 4:10–12)

By "carrying around" the death of Jesus (i.e., by being cross-shaped) we reveal the *life* of Jesus to others. This might sound contradictory, but it is the essence of the "trick" of genuinely missional discipleship. That is, the more we embrace the cross as a paradigm for discipleship, the more alive we become and the more we reveal the life of Jesus. In the minutes before he was assassinated on the balcony of the Lorraine Hotel in Memphis in 1968, Martin Luther King was laughing and joking with his friends and associates, encouraging one to sing one of his favorite spirituals at the meeting they were attending later that night, joking with Jesse Jackson about his clothing choices for the evening, and excitedly anticipating the soul food dinner party they were about to enjoy. Though he carried the death of Jesus with him, acutely aware of the danger he was always in, he still paused on that hotel balcony to laugh at Jackson's hip clothes and to rub his hands with glee at the thought of a big meal or at hearing his favorite song. He was alive and giving life. In fact, earlier in 2 Corinthians Paul had referred to Christians emitting the "smell of death" to some, but the "fragrance of life" to others, at the same time (2 Cor. 2:15–16).

The not-yet-missional train their members to be pious. The missional train their members to be life-givers, transformed by the death of Jesus. When the missional study the life of Jesus, they don't do so only to explore the story of the means by which God allowed us access to him as our Father and friend. They do so to learn about themselves as well. The Gospels aren't just about Jesus, but about us also. N. T. Wright says, "Jesus is lifted up to draw us all to himself, and to enable us to be for the world what he was for the world."[11] The study of the Gospels is the study of the blueprint for our missional discipleship.

For example, when we hear Jesus saying of us that out of our hearts (or more accurately our bellies) "shall flow rivers of living water" (John 7:38 NRSV), he is directly referencing the great prophecy of Ezekiel 47, where water flows from the temple in Jerusalem. In the Ezekiel image, rivers flow from under the threshold of the temple, indicating the life-giving restoration that will come to Israel. Jesus takes this imagery and applies it to his followers—we have become the temple of the living God. From us flow life-giving streams, the life made possible only by the death and resurrection of Jesus. But John 7:38 doesn't only reference our function as the temple of the Spirit of God. It also references the river that flows out of Eden, as described in Genesis 2:10–14. It is a creation image as much as it is a temple image. Now, the rivers of living water that flow out of the temple of God in the new creation bubble up not just from Jesus himself, but from all those who believe in him, who follow him, who become in their turn the channels through which his healing love can flow to the world. This reaches its climax after the resurrection (as I've mentioned a few times now) when Jesus commissions his disciples in John 20:21 ("As the Father has sent me, I am sending you"). He then breathes on his disciples in the same way God breathed life into the nostrils of Adam and Eve (Gen. 2:7), reinforcing the creation motif. They are the new creation, the firstborn of all those followers who are to come. So, although we embrace the death of Jesus and shape our lives, our discipleship, around the paradigm of the cross, we are commissioned as life-bringers, as the temples of God and the new creation. Lesslie Newbigin says,

> Forty times in [John's] Gospel Jesus is described as the one sent by the Father; now he sends them to continue and complete his mission. This mission wholly defines the nature of the church as a body of men and women sent into the public life of the world to be the bearer of that peace which Christ has wrought by the blood of his cross. They will participate in his mission as they participate in his passion.[12]

I suspect we need to develop a greater sense of what cruciform discipleship looks like. Pietistic discipleship is easier to work out. The rules are clear and pietistic churches will brook no dissent. They don't drink, smoke, dance, or chew, or go with girls who do. But cruciformity—a fully engaged approach—takes some finessing. It's a matter of constant vigilance, practice, and yes, trial and error. I think discipling people in a cruciform paradigm will look more like a trade apprenticeship and less like induction into the military. Instead of following orders, it will look like learning to play with new tools and experiencing an emerging confidence and capacity to imitate Jesus in all circumstances. Pietism won't allow trial and error. Well, it won't allow error actually. Cruciformity requires a growing capacity that allows for our getting it wrong or crossing lines occasionally with no fear of condemnation or rejection.

As a young boy I remember being taken along to the local hardware store with my father. It was a dazzling sensory experience. It was an old barn of a building—one big room that smelled of ancient hardwood floorboards, soaked with linseed oil. And its rows of hammers and saws and other unidentifiable tools hanging on the walls and especially the bins of nails, screws, nuts, and bolts of all sizes were a visual feast. For me, it was much better than any toy store. I completely enjoyed just smelling the smells and looking at all the tools in their various shapes and sizes. I didn't feel the need to buy anything, because I was too young to use any of the tools. It was just one of those sensory experiences that stays with you that you long to revisit it but you can't. With the advent of Home Depot, Lowe's, and True Value, the days of "experiencing" the true hardware store are long over. The strip mall is now the wave of the present and future and has little or no aesthetic value, nor do strip malls provide wholesome sensory experiences.

Of course, a trip to the hardware store was never an end in itself. It was a means to a far greater end; once we got all that cool hardware home, it was time to try it all out. Unfortunately, I'm not a natural when it comes to home handyman work. I would bend nails, pound my thumb, cut boards unevenly, cut myself in the process, and whatever I turned out seemed to be a waste of effort, wood, and nails. And yet as discouraging as that all was, for some reason I didn't give up. Even to this day I love old-school hardware stores because they remind me of the joy and excitement of trying out new tools and techniques.

I can't help but think that theological schools have gone the way of the big-box hardware stores. Seminaries can be more akin to Home Depot than my old childhood hardware store. Everyone is in and out as quickly as they can. Instructors give demonstrations on how to use all the great tools, and then we're sent out into the world or into ministry to use the tools we just learned about. But many graduates are not yet adept at using those tools: they bend nails, bang their thumbs, cut uneven boards, and cut themselves. Of course, with your father's old nails and scraps of wood, it's perfectly fine to make such mistakes. But in some churches that kind of experimentation and play is not acceptable. Either it makes the church look unprofessional when it's doing everything to look as attractive as possible, or worse, it could lead to the abuse of people who put their trust in you. The careless use of tools by someone who wasn't given the space and grace to make small, salvageable mistakes early often leads them to make much larger, potentially fatal mistakes in ministry later.

Many of us live in such a hurried and fragmented society that we don't have the time to learn the skills of using God's tools without fumbling around making wobbling three-legged milk stools. For those of us busy in the ministry, when was there time to learn the skills to cultivate the fruit of the Spirit in our own lives? And as ministers, how could we help Jesus' followers do the same if we could not do it for ourselves. Whenever I visit Home Depot, it makes me realize again that many of us never had time to properly nurture the fruit of the Spirit in our lives and so we have been left with pretty serious gaps in our character and our capacity for mission.

More than fifty years ago, philosopher Michael Polanyi wrote about the need to recover an apprentice-master relationship in the passing on of knowledge. Using the great Italian luthier, or violin maker, Antonio Stradivari as an example, Polanyi makes a strong case for what might be referred to as "elbow learning"—the passing on of knowledge that can only occur when sitting at the elbow of a master craftsman. According to their reputation, Stradivari's violins (referred to by the Latinized version of his name, Stradivarius) emit a quality of sound that has defied attempts to explain or reproduce. And yet the Stradivari family never wrote a guide to the creation of a perfect violin. Each instrument was produced by the instinct of the craftsman. Polanyi writes, "It is pathetic to watch the endless efforts—equipped with microscopy and chemistry, with mathematics and electronics—to reproduce a single violin of the kind the half-literate Stradivarius turned out as a matter of routine more than 200 years ago."[13] In other words, some of the most beautiful things confound rules and regulations. They must be *felt*. I would suggest that cruciform discipleship is similar. Pietistic rules cannot contain it. One must feel her way into it. But this is not a process undertaken alone. It must be guided by a master. Polanyi continues,

> To learn by example is to submit to authority. You follow your master because you trust his manner of doing things even when you cannot analyze and account in detail for its effectiveness. By watching the master and emulating his efforts in the presence of his example, the apprentice unconsciously picks up the rules of the art, including those which are not explicitly known to the master himself. These hidden rules can be assimilated only by a person who surrenders himself to that extent uncritically to the imitation of the master.[14]

When creating a violin, Stradivari would carefully choose the required wood, weighing it, feeling its balance, measuring its quality, not by slide rule or guidebook, but in his hands. Then he would bring his apprentice to his elbow and pass him the chosen wood. No apprentice could explain which pieces were chosen and which rejected. They felt it in their hands after learning to feel what their master felt. Is this not exactly what we see Jesus doing with his disciples? He brings them to his elbow and invites them to feel his kingdom work before putting it into practice themselves. As Polanyi concluded, and I paraphrase him here, practical wisdom is more truly embodied in action than expressed in *rules* of action. When Jesus tells his disciples to go and make disciples, "teaching them to obey everything I have commanded you" (Matt. 28:20), he is not simply instructing them to be faithful to his curriculum, but to pass on the "elbow learning" they have received. This is also what I take him to mean in Mark 10:39, when Jesus tells his followers, "You will drink the cup I drink and be baptized with the baptism I am baptized with." Like Stradivari, you will feel what I feel, do as

I do, embody the truth as I have embodied the truth. This kind of learning defies attempts to codify it in legislation.

Just as Stradivari couldn't adequately write down the coordinates for his violins, Jesus' curriculum had to be lived and felt in order for it to be passed on. The cruciform nature of this elbow learning is revealed in John's Gospel when he reports Jesus as saying, "My command is this: Love each other as I have loved you. Greater love has no one than this, that he lay down his life for his friends" (John 15:12–13). In other words, even at the very depth of our sense of Christian community, our love for each other should be cross-shaped, as displayed to us by Jesus.

People who have grown up in the pietistic tradition never got to experiment or play with cruciformity. They had to get all their ducks in a row back in their churchgoing childhood and any mistake, any infraction, was considered a serious offense. What if we saw cruciformity as a lengthy process of development? What if we realized churches and seminaries should be more like the linseed-soaked hardware stores of old and less like Lowe's? What if learning to imitate Jesus happened at the elbow of a master craftsman/missionary and less in the Wednesday night prayer meeting? What if we were allowed to make mistakes and pick ourselves up and dust ourselves off and move forward with even greater resolve? The master craftsman/missionary shows you how to understand your relationship to the alternate reality of the reign of God. As writer and artist Jen Lemen says,

> The leader shows you how not to be too afraid while you do that, how to relax a little, how to plunge ahead into the chaos lighthearted and pull yourself out of the fire unscathed. A leader shows you by living beside you what it means to be terrified yet faithful, doubtful yet full of hope.[15]

BREATHING SHALOM

Bringing Reconciliation, Justice, and Beauty to a Broken World

Hope has two beautiful daughters: Anger, at the
way things are, and Courage, to work for change.

—St. Augustine

In 2010, a pretty eighteen-year-old woman named Alexis Neiers was arrested for being an alleged member of the so-called Bling Ring, an audacious burglary gang in Hollywood that was accused of stealing more than $3 million in clothing and jewelry from the homes of such celebrities as Paris Hilton, Lindsay Lohan, Orlando Bloom, and others. Initially Neiers denied all charges, but she wasn't prepared to let her fifteen minutes of fame slip by too quickly. For her arraignment at Los Angeles Superior Court, Neiers had an *E!* reality show film crew in tow and was mobbed by camera crews from *Good Morning America, Dateline NBC,* and *TMZ.* A former pole-dancing instructor, she was wearing a tweed miniskirt, a pink sweater, and six-inch high-heels. "I have a pretty cool shoe collection going on right now," she inexplicably told awaiting reporters. Earlier, she had been quoted by *Vanity Fair* magazine as saying,

> I'm a firm believer in Karma and I think this situation was attracted into my life because it was supposed to be a huge learning lesson for me to grow and expand as a spiritual being. I see myself being like an Angelina Jolie, but even stronger, pushing even harder for the universe and for peace and for the health of our planet. God didn't give me these talents and looks to just sit around being a model or being famous. I want to lead a huge charity organization. I want to lead a country for all I know.[1]

You can't say the girl doesn't think big. Eighteen-year-old Alexis Neiers, former pole-dancing instructor, now marginally famous for her involvement with members of a burglary gang, is ready to seize her opportunity to change the world. Don't laugh. If Neiers wants to "push even harder for the universe and for peace and for the health of our planet," what's up with all the eighteen-year-olds in church? Where is their passion to change the world? Could it be that they've been convinced by their leaders that God is only concerned about the state of the church, not the world?

I don't need to see another brochure advertising another Christian conference about how to change the church. Surely we have tried every iteration, every permutation, every shape and color that church can be—from the highly liturgical to the congregational, from the emerging to the seeker-oriented, from the Spirit-led to the Calvinist. We have online churches, drive-thru churches, XXX churches, cowboy churches, gay churches, liberal churches, fundamentalist churches. I have worshiped in a student house church in Sao Paulo, and by the swimming pool in a suburban house church in Walnut Creek. I have gathered with believers in a downtown Methodist church in San Francisco with a 100-piece choir swaying and dancing to old-time gospel songs. I have worshiped with Khmer believers in a thatch-roofed shack just outside Phnom Penh. I preached at the four morning services (yes, four—yes, morning!) at First Presbyterian Church, San Antonio. I have participated in a drum circle in a church that meets in a garage-cum-rehearsal space in Los Angeles. I have hung out in Berlin with a church that grew out of the friendships of a Farsi-language jazz quartet. I've attended megachurches, house churches, chapels, cathedrals, and Aboriginal bush services. My point is that we need to just let churches be what God directs them to be in their given setting. There is no final one-size-fits-all blueprint for what a church meeting should look like. We can become obsessed with this discussion, constantly seeking what shape our public meetings should take to attract more attendees and ultimately more followers. What if we spent as much time obsessing about how to change our world, our city, or our neighborhood?

If we really believed that the universal reign of God through Jesus has come and is coming in our neighborhood, where would we spend our time, what would we make our priorities? Let me remind you of the words of Howard Snyder, quoted earlier, "Church people worry that the world might change the church; Kingdom people work to see the church change the world."[2]

Participating in the Coming Kingdom

The reign of God through Christ is a present reality but also an unfolding one. Heaven overlaps with earth. God's reign is complete. Jesus is Lord. These are irrefutable, nonnegotiable, universal truths. But they are truths we perceive only partially. Their full reality is still mysterious to us. One day, "at the regeneration of all things" as Jesus tells us,[3] the reign of God will be understood completely, utterly, unquestioningly. Until that day, we are to participate with God in the mysterious and wonderful work of fashioning foretastes of this world to come. So what exactly might that entail in real terms? In his books *Simply Christian* and *Surprised by Hope*, N. T. Wright suggests three broad elements of this here-and-still-coming reign of God. They are an excellent shorthand way of thinking about how to participate in the coming kingdom, or how to fashion foretastes of the reign of God through Christ.

1. Relationships Restored

The essential outworking of the gospel is peace: peace with God and with each other through Christ. As I mentioned earlier, this idea of *shalom* (peace) is central to the reign of God as confirmed by Jesus' ministry and his commissioning of his earliest followers. When in John 20:21 the resurrected Jesus sends his disciples to continue his mission, he does so by first breathing his shalom into them. Commenting on this, Lesslie Newbigin says,

> Peace (*shalom*), his gift to them, is that which belongs to the new age which God has promised. It is because Jesus bears the wounds of his decisive battle with evil that he has that peace in his gift. He has "made peace by the blood of his cross" (Col. 1:20). But the gift of peace is not for them alone. On the contrary he has chosen and appointed them to be the bearers of shalom into the life of the world.[4]

Shalom means more than the English word "peace" often conveys. It is more than an inner feeling of serenity and calm. It is more than the absence of conflict. It refers to that much-desired state where things are finally made right between us all. Shalom suggests a restoration of relationship between all peoples, as well as reconciliation between humanity and God. It also suggests the restoration of the earth and our relationship to the land. As I mentioned, this can only be understood partially today. We can barely imagine what such a restoration of relationships between ourselves, God, and the earth could look like. But believing in it, we embrace our vocation to announce and demonstrate foretastes of what such restoration might be like.

Because we have peace with God, we are commissioned to demonstrate it to others by making peace with each other and the world. Jesus' marvelous parable of the prodigal son is helpful here. Not only does it reveal the Father's love for his sinful children, but it reaffirms what shalom looks like in the restoration of relationships. Four times throughout the parable the father of the story models what the transformation of anger into grace looks like. Four times he reveals himself to be an example of shalom. First, when the so-called prodigal son initially approaches his father about receiving his inheritance, the father's response would have been astonishing to Jesus' listeners: "There was a man who had two sons. The younger one said to his father, 'Father, give me my share of the estate.' So he divided his property between them" (Luke 15:11–12).

Anyone from the Middle East would know that such a request is the greatest insult that a man could ever give his father. It is unspeakably offensive, and it would be expected by Jesus' listeners that even the most loving father would take to his recalcitrant son with a whip. But in Jesus' story the father, though presumably filled with anger, reprocesses his rage into shalom and agrees to his son's unreasonable request.

Then, when the worthless son has lost everything on dissolute living, it would again be reasonable for the father to respond with unchecked anger, but instead he reprocesses his rage into shalom and welcomes him home: "His father saw him and was filled with compassion for him; he ran to his son, threw his arms around him and kissed him" (v. 20).

Then for a third time the father's commitment to shalom is tested, this time by his older son who refuses to attend his brother's welcome home party (v. 28). The refusal by a son to accept an invitation from his father to a feast, no matter the purpose of the celebration, would have been tantamount to a slap in the face. It was unthinkable. No son would behave this way, even if he did resent his younger brother's behavior. But yet again, the father reveals Jesus' vision for the reign of God, a kingdom of restored relationships, of grace, of shalom: "So his father went out and pleaded with him" (v. 28). Jesus' listeners were probably thinking that the father should have gone out and beat him, not reasoned with him. It is another example of the reprocessing of anger into grace.

The fourth instance of embodied shalom occurs when the father is faced with the out-and-out disrespect of his oldest son in the presence of the household servants and invited guests. In Middle Eastern culture, even if you think your father is making a foolish decision, the last thing you would ever do is question that decision in public. But this son doesn't only question his father, he openly berates him. And yet again, the father who has every right to be outraged by his son responds with grace:

But he answered his father, "Look! All these years I've been slaving for you and never disobeyed your orders. Yet you never gave me even a young goat so I could celebrate with my friends. But when this son of yours who has squandered your property with prostitutes comes home, you kill the fattened calf for him!"

"My son," the father said, "you are always with me, and everything I have is yours. But we had to celebrate and be glad, because this brother of yours was dead and is alive again; he was lost and is found." (vv. 29–32)

Many of us who do not understand the social conventions of the Middle East simply see the father's acceptance of his prodigal son back home as the exemplar of grace that we are to take from Jesus' parable. But those who do understand such conventions know that Jesus is layering his story with multiple examples of the father's forgiveness and the restoration of relationships. Four times the father subdues his very understandable and reasonable anger and converts it into the grace-filled response of shalom. And by so doing he reveals that restored relationships are only maintained by costly demonstrations of unexpected love.

It has often been noted that the parable of the prodigal son is like the gospel within the Gospels. It is Jesus' most explicit description of the doctrine that would later be called salvation by grace. And it reveals that in the atonement—the costly death of Jesus on the cross—God the Father is reprocessing his anger into grace. God takes on the punishment himself. He demonstrates his commitment to shalom with humankind by the costly demonstration of love revealed in the cross. Not only does this create the means by which we, like prodigals, can have peace with God, but it reveals again a framework for Christian mission. We must reprocess our anger into grace. We must show shalom in costly demonstrations of unexpected love. This is what it looks like to cooperate with the universal reign of God. As we noted earlier, in the words of Lesslie Newbigin, God has chosen and appointed us to be the bearers of shalom into the life of the world through acts of unexpected love.

I heard recently of a law-abiding, middle-class family in Edmonton, Canada, whose son had broken their hearts by becoming involved in gang activity, including the drugs and crime that go along with it. One day he witnessed a serious crime conducted by a rival gang member whose identity was well known to him. The rival gang was concerned that he might go to the police with the information he had, so they drove by his family home one night and shot up the house as a warning to him to remain silent. As you can imagine, the quiet suburban community in which they lived was outraged that this family was bringing gangs into their neighborhood. When a second drive-by shooting occurred at the house, narrowly missing the family inside, the neighbors began to mutter among themselves. They wanted the family out of their suburb. Because the boy's family was only renting the house, their neighbors began a whisper campaign that they should consider moving away. Try to imagine the horror this family was dealing with. They were already beside themselves with worry for their son and brother. Now they were terrified for their own lives. And to make matters worse, they knew their neighbors were turning against them.

Two Christian families in that suburb, however, saw that reconciled relationships were an evidence of the reign of God. They were not willing to let this horrified family slip away to face their demons alone somewhere else. They arranged a community meeting and managed to convince their neighbors that this was no way to treat people in such a dreadful situation. Together with their neighbors they developed a series of strategies for protecting each other (neighborhood watch patrols, curfews for children, and so forth) and then they approached the terrorized family with gifts and expressed the whole community's concern for them, letting them know that they didn't want them to move away, and telling them they would stand with them no matter what. This is what it looks like when the redeemed ones cooperate with the universal reign of God in their neighborhood. It is evidenced by reconciliation, hospitality, and generosity, no matter how costly. We reprocess our anger—or in this case, fear—into grace and express that through costly demonstrations of love.

And this work is needed more than ever in society. In 2006, the *American Sociological Review* completed a survey on the importance of friendship in people's lives in order to compare this with the 1985 findings of the General Social Survey (GSS). Back in '85, the GSS asked participants to number their "close friends" and found that respondents were likely to claim three—often noting that these relationships were based in their neighborhood or local community. Twenty years later, the *American Sociological Review* published their findings, which showed a threefold increase in the number of Americans who didn't have anyone with whom to discuss important matters. Specifically they found that nearly one-quarter of the 1,500 participants claimed they had no confidants at all. Half had two or fewer close friends. It was concluded that

> Americans are in effect getting lonelier. In 1985 the best means we had to "reach out and touch someone" was the telephone. For all the advances in communications since then—cellular phones, the Internet, instant messages, email, chat rooms, social networking sites—we now feel more isolated.[5]

Surely, more than ever, the kingdom work of reconciled relationships, renewed neighborhoods, and closer friendships will demonstrate the reign of God through Christ in the here and now.

2. Justice Reestablished

The second broad evidence of the reign of God on earth is the reestablishment of justice within human society. Technically one could argue that justice is an expression of restored relationships, but I think it is nonetheless helpful to separate it for examination in its own right. Shalom cannot just describe our individual relationships with God and others; it should also describe the emergence of a loving and just society at a more corporate level. And it is one of the most common descriptions of the kingdom of God we find in the Old Testament. Indeed, when the prophets of Israel and Judah dream of what the coming kingdom will be like, they never express it as some kind of individualized hope for eternal life. They speak of the reestablishment of a just and equitable society on earth. For example, in the beginning of the book of Isaiah we find the prophet voicing Yahweh's displeasure with the remnant nation of Judah and its capital, Jerusalem, and yearning for a day when heaven and earth overlap and God's reign is revealed once and for all. He begins his prophecy with the triumphant, "Hear, O heavens! Listen, O earth! For the Lord has spoken" (Isa. 1:2), demonstrating his recognition that the word of Yahweh speaks into both realms because he intends for them one day to be united. The rest of chapter 1 is an inventory of Judah's sin—their rebellious leaders, government corruption, injustice and oppression, empty worship and idolatry. Judah doesn't do what is right, she doesn't "seek justice, rescue the oppressed, defend the orphan, plead for the widow" (v. 17 NRSV). And as a result, Isaiah depicts Yahweh as alternately angry, annoyed, weary, frustrated, and impatient with Judah and Jerusalem. But then, at the beginning of chapter 2, the prophet launches into Yahweh's desire for a coming kingdom, a world freed from this kind of sin and injustice:

> In the last days
> the mountain of the LORD's temple will be established
>   as chief among the mountains;
> it will be raised above the hills,
>   and all nations will stream to it.
> Many peoples will come and say,
> "Come, let us go up to the mountain of the LORD,
>   to the house of the God of Jacob.
> He will teach us his ways,
>   so that we may walk in his paths."
> The law will go out from Zion,
>   the word of the LORD from Jerusalem.
> He will judge between the nations
>   and will settle disputes for many peoples.
> They will beat their swords into plowshares
>   and their spears into pruning hooks.
> Nation will not take up sword against nation,
>   nor will they train for war anymore. (Isa. 2:2–4)

Such a prophecy coming on the back of Yahweh's complaints about the conduct of his people is not rare in the Old Testament. There are many similar examples. This one is quoted simply as an exemplar of such prophecies, and as such it reveals the kind of kingdom that God promises to his people over and over. It is a kingdom of restored relationships and reestablished justice. The key elements of God's universal reign revealed in this passage include:

- Complete unmediated access to the truth of God ("He will teach us his ways . . . The law will go out from Zion, the word of the LORD from Jerusalem.")
- Empowered righteous living ("so that we may walk in his paths.")

- International justice ("He will judge between the nations and will settle disputes for many peoples.")
- Global peace ("Nation will not take up sword against nation, nor will they train for war anymore.")

Of course, the original author cannot begin to conceive of what this universal reign of God might look like. Grasping for an image to describe the coming day of the Lord, all he can do is depict it as the reestablishment of Zion as the preeminent mountaintop temple of Yahweh. He says, "The mountain of the LORD's temple will be established as chief among the mountains; it will be raised above the hills, and all nations will stream to it" (v. 2). But we know that in Christ the universal reign has been established beyond Mount Zion and indeed beyond the borders of Judah or Israel. The future house of God, of which Isaiah speaks, turned out not to be a new temple, but the incarnation of God in the human form of Jesus. So, it's not literally a new mountain, as Isaiah describes, and about which Jews were to debate long and hard. This is why a Samaritan woman questions Jesus about whether Yahweh should be worshiped on Zion as the Jews believed or on Mount Gerizim as the Samaritans believed. But Jesus' response is, "Believe me, woman, a time is coming when you will worship the Father neither on this mountain nor in Jerusalem" (John 4:21). Indeed, that time was when humankind would worship the Father through the Son anywhere and everywhere. When Jesus says, "I am able to destroy the temple of God and rebuild it in three days" (Matt. 26:61), we know he is speaking not of any building on Mount Zion, but of his own body. *He* is the temple of God. In him heaven and earth are made to overlap, and the world that results is one of global peace and international justice.

The truly missional among us are committed to cooperating with the universal reign of God to see traces of this coming kingdom of justice revealed in the here and now. A commitment to justice cannot ever be relegated to the theoretical. It must be made practical, in relationship, with the poor. As theologian priest Gustavo Gutiérrez once pointedly remarked, "You say you care about the poor. Then tell me, what are their names?"[6] Here we see the intersection of restored relationships and reestablished justice. Justice without relationship is hardly justice at all. Multnomah professors Brad Harper and Paul Louis Metzger make this powerful challenge:

> The church is a community of people called to relocate, reconcile, and redistribute its wealth on behalf of all people—inside and outside the church, especially the downtrodden—for Jesus' sake. The church that relocates, reconciles, and redistributes wealth in this way moves out as a missional witness to the communal and co-missional God, who wages war against the whore of Babylon and the merchants with whom she committed adultery, and against Pharaoh and Caesar, who impose their nameless deity and imperial rule on peoples for their own economic gain. This missional church prefigures the day when the city of the New Jerusalem—Christ's holy bride—will [appear].[7]

3. Beauty Rediscovered

Third, N. T. Wright is correct when he says that the overlapping of heaven and earth will be evidenced by the rediscovery of redeemed beauty. In a world stained by sin and rebellion, beauty is often reduced to the sexually alluring, but in the here-and-still-coming kingdom, beauty is redeemed and becomes a sign of the universal reign of God. After all, aren't all people drawn to true beauty? Isn't it a kind of universal yearning? Whether it is great music, art, architecture, or nature, humankind recognizes the intrinsic and spiritual value of beauty. Little wonder then that Wright identifies it as an expression of the world to come. We are drawn so powerfully to beauty and unwittingly then to the God of all beauty. Great artists understand this. It is why the painter Vincent Van Gogh could say, "When I have a terrible need of—shall I say the word—religion, then I go out and paint the stars."[8] Or in a similar vein, the Icelandic singer Bjork says, "All Icelandic people are nature-lovers. If they have problems, they can't handle work or relationships, they will go for a walk on a mountain, and they'll come back and it'll be fine. It's the same occasions when, if you were a Catholic, you'd go to church."[9] An encounter with the beauty of nature draws us to the Creator of all beauty in the knowledge that in the world to come the earth will be redeemed to its pristine form. As Paul says, "The creation waits in eager expectation for the sons of God to be revealed" (Rom. 8:19).

Therefore, any encounter with the beauty and splendor of creation is an encounter with a sign from its Creator. Those of us who take this by faith ought to be all the more drawn to see God in nature. The Christian mystic and theologian Evelyn Underhill said over seventy years ago, "When we are awed by the intolerable majesty of the Himalaya, we are merely receiving through symbols adapted to our size, intimations of the Absolute beauty." In appreciating objects of true beauty, Underhill believed we pass "through and beyond this object, to the experience of the Absolute revealed in things."[10]

But even beautiful objects created by humankind can be appreciated in this way. The atheist Anthony O'Hear admits as much when he says, "Through art, particularly the great masterpieces of the past, we do have intimations of beauty, of order, *of divinity even*" (italics added).[11] Those of us who have embraced faith in the universal reign of God through Christ look for expressions of beauty everywhere, whether they be a stunning sunset, a painting by a grand master, a gorgeous piece of music, or a delicious meal. I think the primary way they lead us back to God is through the profound sense of gratitude one feels when partaking of such beauty. G. K. Chesterton was noted to have quipped that the worst moment for an atheist is when he or she feels deeply grateful yet has no one to thank. This, it seems, is what O'Hear is saying. Great art leads us to be grateful that we are able to view it, no matter the motivations or beliefs of the artist. We can be drawn toward the reign of God through beautiful sacred music but also through the music of dubious characters like Mozart, McCartney, and Led Zeppelin. That's because beauty is a sign of the kingdom of God, and it draws from us a desire for more of its beauty, its order, its divinity.

Beauty, Justice, Relationship

I have had the opportunity to visit a number of the buildings designed by the great American architect Frank Lloyd Wright. From the Robie House, his very early masterpiece in the prairie style he made famous in Hyde Park, Chicago, to his home and studio down the road in Oak Park, to the astonishing Fallingwater in Mill Run, Pennsylvania, Wright's private residences are remarkable works of art. But they are also family spaces, created to promote harmony and peace among those who lived there. In the dining rooms of all three of these houses, the chairs have tall, straight backs that rise up above the heads of those who sit in them. Wright designed the chairs so that the families who use them would be brought together around the dining table. The high chair backs create an extra wall—a room within a room to enclose the family around the table. Similarly, he included a servery through the wall from the kitchen to the dining room so that servants wouldn't interrupt the family time of those at the table.

But more important than the dining room for Wright was the fireplace. In each of these houses the hearth is the centerpiece of the building. This is especially so in Fallingwater, where the hearth is literally the smoothed top of the massive boulder on which the building is anchored. It's as if Wright was telling us in his design that time around the fire was the anchor of family life. Wandering around Fallingwater I was stunned by the beauty of this amazing, iconic building, and its harmony with the stream, the waterfall, and the forest by which it is situated. It is an expression of true beauty—promoting shalom between its residents themselves and between them and the countryside around them. Although he didn't know it (or I suspect he didn't know it), Wright was tapping into our yearnings for beauty, justice, and relationship, and his private residences all express dimensions of these aspects of the kingdom.

The interesting thing about Wright's vision for the family life of his clients is that he knew very little about shalom—beauty, justice, relationship—in his own private life. In 1909, while the Robie House was still being built, he left his wife Kitty and their six children for Mameh Cheney, the wife of one of his clients. Wright and Cheney moved to Wisconsin and lived together until 1914 when she was murdered by a religious fanatic outraged that she was living in sin with the great architect. The following year, Wright began a relationship with Miriam Noel that lasted until 1922 when Kitty granted him a divorce and he and Miriam were finally married. But six months after the ceremony, the fifty-seven-year-old Wright had an affair with twenty-six-year-old Olgivanna Hinzenburg, a married mother-of-one who then bore him a daughter in 1925. Miriam Noel then sued Wright for "alienation of affections," and while she eventually granted him a divorce in 1927, the whole tawdry affair exacted a dreadful toll on her. She went insane and died in a psychiatric hospital in 1930. As David Dale says, rather flippantly, "The most influential architect of the 20th century believed in the family, which is why he had so many of them."[12]

But Frank Lloyd Wright was onto something. He had sensed something beautiful and true about the nature of family, and he had incorporated a belief in these things into his amazing designs. In this respect I would say he strayed into the values of God's reign without necessarily submitting to them. His buildings should be appreciated for the way they demonstrate the beauty and the values of the kingdom, whether he was conscious of their source or not. So it need not only be in the beautiful simplicity of Mennonite quilting that we look for traces of God's reign. It can be found in the serene panels of Mark Rothko, the superbly crafted sentences of Ernest Hemingway or the passionate lyrics of Bob Dylan, the soaring symphonies of Beethoven, or the spiritually anguished songs of Leonard Cohen. None of these people might acknowledge the universal reign of God, but where we encounter beauty through their work, we experience gratitude, and when we experience gratitude, we need the Creator of all beauty to be its object. Where we sense their yearning for justice and love, we can sense their desire for the reign of God, whether consciously or unconsciously. And we should devote ourselves, as persons of faith, to unfurling glimpses of beauty, justice, and love in our world by the means most appropriate to our circumstances, gifts, abilities, and desires.

Therefore, designing great buildings can be an expression of mission. Creating great art or music can also be, because they are cooperating with the unfurling reign of God. The following quotation, attributed to the Reformer Martin Luther, describes this,

> The maid who sweeps her kitchen is doing the will of God just as much as the monk who prays—not because she may sing a Christian hymn as she sweeps but because God loves clean floors. The Christian shoemaker does his Christian duty not by putting little crosses on the shoes, but by making good shoes, because God is interested in good craftsmanship.

If we truly want to change the world, not just the church, we must understand that it is our task to commit ourselves to relational reconciliation, to justice and peace, and to good craftsmanship. The missional Christian community should be at the forefront of relational reconciliation, as it was in the early years of post-apartheid South Africa. The missional Christian community should be committed to the creation of a more just society, as it was in the launch of Micah Challenge and the Millennium Development Goals, aimed at holding the UN to its commitment to end extreme poverty. And the missional Christian community should be creators and purveyors of true beauty, whether it be great art, great music, great architecture, or great shoes. I would also want to add that not only should missional Christians appreciate the beauty of nature, but they should actively participate in its protection. Creation care could be seen as an expression of the shalom of the kingdom (reconciliation with God, others, *and the earth*) as well as an appreciation of beauty. No matter the category, it is part of our work and duty as missional ones to protect and care for the environment.[13] Instead of focusing so much on what shape our church services should take, what kind of world would we fashion if we saw it as our mission to reconcile relationship, reestablish justice, and rediscover beauty? As N. T. Wright sums it up,

> We are called to be part of God's new creation, called to be agents of that new creation here and now. We are called to model and display that new creation in symphonies and family life, in restorative justice and poetry, in holiness and service to the poor, in politics and painting.[14]

Changing the World

Recently, many seminars on missional living have been making much of Jesus' commissioning of seventy-two of his disciples to go out in pairs into the world to fulfill his mission (Luke 10:1–17). I can see why this passage has been rediscovered by missional thinkers and practitioners. It is certainly about Jesus sending his followers out, and it contains clues to the nature of the missional church. For example, one could deduce from this passage that mission is a communal venture (he "sent them two by two"—v. 1); mission involves an announcement of the reign of God (Jesus tells them to announce "The kingdom of God is near you"—v. 8); mission is anchored in the shalom of God's rule (he tells them to say, "Peace to this house"—v. 5); mission is a risky venture and can attract opposition (he commissions them with, "I am sending you out like lambs among wolves"—v. 3). Indeed, we have already explored these aspects of mission. Luke 10 also forms the basis for the idea of finding "persons of peace," those who are open to the reign of God through Christ, and with whom we need to spend more of our time (see v. 6).

But one further aspect often teased out by missional seminar presenters is that in Luke 10 Jesus instructs his disciples to take no purse or bag or sandals for the journey (v. 4). I have heard it often suggested that the reason for this is to keep his disciples humble, to force them to rely on the kindness of the strangers to whom they've been sent. This is seen as an example of Jesus insisting that his followers adopt a dependent posture toward others rather than lording it over them. There is some sense in this and Jesus certainly was insistent that his followers not throw their weight around like other leaders in society were inclined to do. But this is not what Jesus is doing in this instance. Any Jewish listener to Jesus' instructions about purses, bags, and sandals would have immediately recognized that these are the very same instructions given to those worshipers who approach the Temple Mount in Jerusalem. Jesus is sending his disciples out into the world, like a faithful Jewish pilgrim would prepare to worship Yahweh on his mountain. The symbolism is unmistakable. All of Israel's and Judah's hope for the future house of God, as prophesied in Old Testament passages like the Isaiah 2 verses we looked at earlier, are being fulfilled in the mission of Jesus. And this mission is not located on Mount Zion, but in the households to whom the disciples have been sent. Recall again Jesus' words to the woman at the well in John 4:21: "A time is coming when you will worship the Father neither on this mountain nor in Jerusalem." By sending his disciples out into the mission field like penitent worshipers approaching the Temple Mount, he is saying that the world is not his parish, but the world is his *temple*.

The not-yet-missional still see the church building as the temple of Jesus and therefore they are deeply concerned about getting what goes on in there as correct as possible. They refer to that building as the "sanctuary." They try to encourage the faithful to revere their sanctuary in the same way that Israel revered their temple. Indeed, this is the same way many religious communities revere their holy places of worship, whether mosques, temples, wats, shrines, basilicas, or cathedrals. But in instituting his mission through the sending out of the seventy-two, Jesus implies a complete and utter worldview shift. Now, every household, every village, every town and city is the dwelling place of God. Heaven and earth now overlap through the incarnation and the whole earth has become the holy domain of the Triune God. Going out without a purse or bag or sandals to announce that the kingdom of God is near is an act of worship. It is cooperation with the universal reign of God through Christ. This reign is demonstrated in reconciled relationships, justice and peace, a renewed environment, great food, great art and music, indeed great craftsmanship of every kind. And it involves an alerting of all people to the fact of history that our God reigns. It is world-changing, not just church-changing.

And we know full well that this world needs changing. This is the world where a child dies from hunger and curable disease every three seconds; where 8,500 people die from AIDS and another 13,000 contract HIV every day; where an estimated 246 million children are trapped in child labor, and where over one billion people subsist on less than $1 a day. This is a world where one billion people exist in slums, one billion lack access to clean water, and 2.6 billion lack toilets and other forms of basic sanitation.

This is the world in which genocide has become a regular occurrence, including as recently as 1994 when an estimated 800,000 tribal Tutsis were massacred by the rival tribe, the Hutus, in Rwanda, and in 1995 when more than 8,000 Muslim Bosnian men and boys were killed, as well as the ethnic cleansing of 25,000 to 30,000 refugees in Srebrenica by Serbian forces.

This is the world that was changed forever by a series of coordinated suicide attacks on the United States by al-Qaeda operatives using hijacked aircraft on September 11, 2001, resulting in a death toll of 2,995, including the 19 hijackers.

This is the world that is still reeling after the 2004 Asian tsunami wiped out 230,000 people in Indonesia, Thailand, Sri Lanka, and

India in a single deadly wave, and where the Haiti earthquake killed 250,000 in 2010.

This is the world still stunned by the 2010 Gulf of Mexico oil spill in which BP's Deepwater Horizon drilling rig dumped hundreds of millions of gallons of oil into the gulf at a rate of something like 50,000 barrels of crude oil every day.

We might feel as though we can't do anything about these enormous issues in our world, but we can act to change the worlds in which we live, believing that our concerted efforts will create a tipping point for justice, reconciliation, and beauty. In Seattle, my friends Ben and Cherie Katt are doing just that through launching an incarnational community in the Aurora neighborhood called Awake. For many in Seattle, Aurora is nothing more than a boundary to cross to get to Green Lake, a road to be used to get downtown or as a debatable short-cut to the airport. As Ben describes it, Aurora was not a destination; it was a gash down the middle of an otherwise vibrant area.

But after he and Cherie moved in, they noticed something in Aurora they'd never really seen before. They started noticing the cheap motels and the rusty cargo vans and RVs parked on the side streets. And they began to realize that many people actually called these decrepit places home. Soon, they began showing up at the sleazy-looking motels to share food with their newly discovered neighbors, and as they listened to their stories, they not only heard the typical and infamous motel stories of drug use and violence, but more often than not they heard from people who simply didn't know where they were going to sleep tomorrow night. They also heard from motel managers who had to function as social workers, trying to accommodate desperate people.

Addictions, unemployment, injury, and mental illness had all contributed to putting them into substandard motel rooms or, worse, in the aging trucks and vans parked on Aurora side streets. Even those with a steady income couldn't afford the housing costs of other Seattle neighborhoods.

The Katts began with a weekly community meal in the small community garden on the corner of Aurora Avenue and 90th Street, an intersection known as "the switchblade" because of all the prostitution, drug dealing, and other criminal activity that happened there.

Today, anywhere between 50 and 100 neighbors gather for a meal hosted by the crew from Awake. But each week, Ben and Cherie kept hearing more tales of woe from people forced to live in cars, motel rooms, and vans due to overwhelming personal circumstances. They knew they had to do something to help, so they decided to attempt their own neighborhood-generated solution.

In 2010, they started the Vacancy Project, an attempt to partner with their homeless neighbors in the Aurora area to help them escape the cycle of poverty and transition into stable, affordable housing. The Vacancy Project provides individuals and families with small no-interest loans to help them cover their rent and a security deposit, in the hope that they will be able to break through what is otherwise an insurmountable barrier in the journey out of homelessness. So far, they've been able to assist a number of families and individuals as they courageously embark on this journey. Ben describes a couple of the families they have helped:

> We provided funds from the Vacancy Project to keep an Eritrean refugee family off the street as they waited for space at an emergency shelter to open up. The family had previously sought help from a variety of organizations but was on the verge of homelessness until an aware motel manager thought of the Vacancy Project and contacted us. Then, a few months ago some of my friends had the privilege of visiting a family that had received a $700 loan from the Vacancy Project shortly after they moved into their new rental home in Lynnwood. My friends brought mattresses for the two little girls—who until then had been sleeping on the floor—and covered them with fresh bed sheets and purple comforters; one with flowers, the other with polka dots. The girls were ecstatic. They stood on the beds and talked about how tall they were. They sat on their beds and tried out every corner. They invited each other over to their respective beds and posed for pictures. I imagine they slept really well that night.[15]

Of course, outdoor community meals don't work so well in a Seattle winter, so just south of 90th on Aurora, and within a few blocks of where most of them live, Ben and the Awake community launched a 1500-square-foot community center called the Aurora Sharehouse. It will be a lot like the garden, only indoors—a place for storytelling and celebrations as well as a hub for neighbors, businesses, faith communities, and other groups to scheme together about how they can build what Ben calls "a continuum of care" to help even more homeless neighbors vacate their vehicles and motel rooms for stable, affordable housing. In their small, localized way, Awake is changing the world without asking any questions about what changes need to be made by the church.

I began this chapter by quoting Alexis Neiers and her desire to "push even harder for the universe and for peace and for the health of our planet" and asking why so many church leaders aren't as ambitious in their desire to change the world. As quoted earlier, Neiers rather immodestly says, "God didn't give me these talents and looks to just sit around being a model or being famous." Well, mightn't we say (although much more modestly) God didn't give us these talents and gifts and all this freedom and initiative just to sit around discussing how to produce a slicker and more impressive worship gathering. He gave us these gifts so that we might breathe shalom throughout the world, that we might bring reconciliation and joy, peace and justice to a broken world yearning for redemption. He gave us these gifts so that we might design beautiful buildings, produce beautiful art, defend and protect this beautiful earth. He gave us these gifts so that we would defend the oppressed and protect the widow and the orphan, and so that we might announce the beautiful message that through Christ our God reigns and that he has defeated sin and death and the devil and that he has come to your house offering you relationship with him and citizenship in a brand-new world that is here and still coming.

MOVING INTO THE NEIGHBORHOOD

Living Out Incarnational Mission

Love your neighbors—not the neighbors you
pick out but the ones you have.

—Wendell Berry

nother of my great theological mentors is Kenneth Bailey, author of such works as *Jesus Through Middle Eastern Eyes*, and his classics, *Through Peasant Eyes* and *Poet and Peasant*.[1] He is an exceptional biblical scholar whose work has profoundly shaped my understanding of Jesus. But above all his scholarship, Ken Bailey is a missionary who spent over sixty years living in the Middle East. He grew up in Egypt and then spent forty years teaching New Testament studies in Egypt, Lebanon, Jerusalem, and Cyprus. While there, he didn't simply take his Western understanding of Jesus to the Middle

East, but allowed the Eastern cultural milieu to shape his studies in the Gospels. He has passed those insights on to the rest of us through his published work, but it is important to remember they have emerged in the context of a lifelong incarnational missional stance.

Given the almost continual unrest in the Middle East, serving in Lebanon was no picnic, but Bailey refused to pull out. When fellow Presbyterian missionary Ben Weir was kidnapped off the streets of Beirut in May 1984, the US government sent in the Marines to evacuate the remaining Americans. But Ken Bailey remained. He respectfully refused the offer of escape and continued about his business. The next day, he realized that the simple act of standing in the bread line under shelling is an incarnational witness. His Lebanese neighbors were astonished to see him. They knew he had the opportunity to flee, as had all the other Americans in the city, and they were deeply moved by his refusal to do so. As Bailey once said to me, when the going gets tough, mere presence is a powerful expression of mission.

I was once taken to task by a very earnest young seminarian who thought references to being *incarnational* were blasphemous, implying as they did (in his mind) that we diminish the importance of *the* Incarnation of Christ by claiming equality with it in his followers. This is to take the term too literally. Those of us calling for an incarnational framework for mission are not making claims for any pseudo-divinity of Jesus' followers. We mean by the term what Kenneth Bailey exemplified in his life. Put simply, we understand it as Princeton professor and missional thinker Darrell Guder summarized over ten years ago:

> By incarnational mission I mean the understanding and practice of Christian witness that is rooted in and shaped by the life, ministry, suffering, death and resurrection of Jesus. The critical question that motivates this study is this: can and should the unique event of the incarnation of Jesus that constitutes and defines the message and mission of the church have concrete significance for the way in which the church communicates that message and carries out that mission?[2]

And I would answer yes it can and yes it should. The call to become incarnational is not the same as the New Age aspiration to contemporary divinity. It is an attempt to live out the firm belief that, as Guder suggests, the Jesus event not only defines the message and mission of the church but shows us *how* to embody and communicate that message and mission.

Moving into the Neighborhood (Proximity)

Eugene Peterson's *The Message* paraphrases John 1:14 as, "The Word became flesh and blood, and *moved into the neighborhood*" (italics added). Incarnational mission means moving into the lives of those to whom we believe we've been sent. Living in one neighborhood, working in another, playing in another, and churching in yet another doesn't model to people that Jesus is willing to move into their neighborhoods. It says that if Jesus' followers don't want to live here, neither would Jesus. The not-yet-missional miss this. They don't take the spiritual geography of neighborhood seriously enough. They are willing to drive their gas-guzzling SUVs halfway across town to attend church, unconcerned about a) those who live in their own neighborhood, or b) those who live in the church's neighborhood. They forget that the very least we can say about the example of Jesus is that proximity is an essential element. This is all the more obvious when it comes to poorer or less desirable neighborhoods, where the residents already feel marginalized from mainstream society, only to have this feeling reinforced by the absence of Christian neighbors. Where there are churches in neighborhoods that have undergone cultural or economic changes in their makeup over the years, often the members of these churches live elsewhere. The church then just becomes an impersonal center for the delivery of Christian services, not a collective of incarnational neighbors. John Perkins describes the outcome of such a situation:

> All too often, we think of the church simply as a building with programs aimed at making sure the church survives and thrives. On this model, people do everything possible to keep the show going. This view of the church is not missional. And as far as the poor in the surrounding community are concerned, they are viewed simply as a side issue—simply the beneficiaries of our charity. In some cases, we may actually go so far as to invite these beneficiaries of our charity to church. But charity does not build community. It fosters dependence

on the one hand and separation on the other hand—keeping the poor at the far end of our outstretched hand.[3]

Recently I was in Toronto, Canada, where I met Nigel Barham, a young man trying to counteract all this nonincarnational ministry. And he is doing so with a deceptively simple plan. All he does is challenge young people to physically relocate, to move into the neighborhood to which they feel called. For Nigel, mission doesn't mean just visiting a neighborhood, even if we visit regularly and provide great Christian services while we're there. For him, incarnational mission means to literally move in. His organization is called just that: MoveIn. All he asks is for people to form into small teams (four to six people), identify a needy, poor, or disadvantaged neighborhood, and then move in and pray for the community for one night per week. Move in and pray. That's it. That's his whole strategy. And young Canadian Christians are signing up in droves. He is currently mobilizing more teams than he can manage. Nigel has no preferred model of church, no strict rule of life, no menu of prefabricated ministries. Simply move in and pray. Let God make use of your presence, your proximity, and your prayer. Furthermore, he believes that because middle-class and wealthy suburban neighborhoods have a surfeit of churches, the preference must be for poor and disadvantaged communities. He writes,

> It is time for Christians to move into neighborhoods because they are not safe—to move into neighborhoods that are messy and have high crime rates, high poverty rates, low standards of living, and a disproportionate representation of Christ. It is also time for those who move into lower-needs neighborhoods to do so on purpose—prayerfully, seriously, communally.[4]

And Barham isn't asking anything he's not willing to do himself. He lives in a two-bedroom apartment with three other young men in a poorer Toronto suburb. Most of his neighbors are Islamic immigrants or asylum seekers from the Middle East. He and his roommates go about their normal business. They have jobs and hobbies and friends like everyone else. The unique thing about them is that they have chosen to live in the place to which they think God has specifically sent them. They then spend one night a week praying for their community, for their immediate neighbors, and for God's guidance. They believe that through prayer and proximity their neighbors will experience Christ's love themselves in a life-changing, life-giving, and contagious kind of way. And it's happening. In a private email to me, he reported,

> Today was an exciting day in my neighborhood. Our "person of peace," actually a Muslim-background Sudanese single mother, suggested we host a BBQ in the park. We invited our friends—mostly single-mother Muslim families—and had a blast together. About 40 of us. Many coming to Christ, slowly, over the weeks and months—mostly through, it seems, neighbors' attraction to our feeble attempts to love one another as we love our neighbor. It's our one-year anniversary. What better way to celebrate?

Note that Barham's approach is about building partnerships with his neighbors, not simply being service providers. As John Perkins said earlier, charity does not build community. At the time of this writing, six other MoveIn households have started across Canada and there are plans for fifteen others, including in the US. Young people are choosing to simply move in and pray. This isn't dissimilar to the work of the Eden network, an English ministry that mobilizes young adults to relocate into public housing estates as a missional initiative.[5] What is going on when the call to relocate among the poor, the lost, the marginalized, is an unusual thing? Isn't that meant to be the way of the followers of Jesus? This is incarnational mission because it imitates the unique event of the incarnation of Jesus. It allows the example of Jesus to not only define the message of the church but to shape the way in which that message is communicated and the way the church carries out its mission. Australian missiologist Ross Langmead explains this further:

> Mission can be labeled incarnational in the sense of (1) being patterned on the incarnation, (2) being enabled by the continuing power of the incarnation, and (3) joining the ongoing incarnating mission of God.[6]

Langmead then teases these three dimensions out, restating them and describing them under three broad categories. I intend to use his categories in my discussion of incarnational mission. Those categories I have summarized as:

- *The following of Christ*—more than mere exemplarism, this involves integrating word and deed, patterned on the life of Jesus, including solidarity with the poor, vulnerable love, and a risky challenge to the status quo.
- *The participation in Christ*—an emphasis on the continuing presence and initiative of the risen Christ, without which discipleship is impossible.
- *Joining in God's incarnational mission*—a commitment to continually reach out as God does, to partner with him in the unfurling of his kingdom.

The Following of Christ (Presence)

As Langmead says, the following of Jesus' example moves beyond mere exemplarism. Jesus is not simply our hero or our guru. He is Lord. It is his reign that forms the framework for all Christian mission. We embrace incarnational mission when we follow the model of ministry revealed to us in Jesus. Darrell Guder suggests that Jesus not only shows us *what* the message and mission is, but *how* it is to be communicated:

> In the New Testament and beginning with Jesus' earthly ministry, God's love was expressed in understandable ways. The Word became flesh so that flesh might encounter and respond to it. . . . Jesus translated the message of the kingdom into a language that could be grasped by a tax collector and a prostitute, a leper and a Samaritan, a learned Pharisee and uneducated fishermen.[7]

Mission consists not only in incarnating the message of Jesus, but in embodying the means by which he presented that message. This moves beyond simply contextualizing the message or aiming at greater cultural relevance. It invites the missionary to live as Jesus lived, to represent his presence with others, not in the hope of gaining Jesus' approval or winning his favor, but as a response to his grace and mercy to us. It is our nonnegotiable missional lifestyle. As rock singer Bono says, "Love has to become an action or something concrete. . . . There must be an incarnation. Love must be made flesh."[8] When he says this we know he is talking in distinctly

Christian terms, citing the example of Jesus without necessarily using his name.

As we saw earlier, Jesus invites his first followers into this kind of missional existence when he commends peace, shalom—the stuff of his kingdom—to them, only to encounter them after his resurrection and do the same. But now, after his resurrection, he does more than commend peace to them, he confers it as the indwelling of the living God: "Again Jesus said, 'Peace be with you! As the Father has sent me, I am sending you.' And with that he breathed on them and said, 'Receive the Holy Spirit'" (John 20:21–22). This is in many ways a superior "commission" to that of Matthew 28 because it tells us not only the fact of our being sent, but the nature of the sending—in the way of Jesus. We are sent in the same manner that the Father sent the Son. And in what manner did he do that? The Son lived for thirty years in the irreligious, rough-and-ready environment of Nazareth, a place from which nothing good was supposed to have come. Thirty years in Galilee, three years of public ministry, his humiliation, his death on the cross. This is the way of mission, according to Jesus' example.

For this reason, many missiologists aren't too keen on short-term mission trips. While these short-term trips are designed to give people a "taste" of cross-cultural mission in the hope that they will create an appetite for a whole life of mission, often they have the reverse effect. Short-term mission trips can inoculate team members against a life of mission by giving them the impression that either a) two weeks in Haiti every few years satisfies the missionary call on their lives, or b) mission is something that only really happens "over there" in Haiti. But Jesus' life was not a short-term mission trip. Incarnational missionaries move into the neighborhood and they stay. Like Kenneth Bailey in Lebanon they stick it out in the good times and the bad. They don't see mission as a quick fix. It's not just one triumphant evangelistic conversation on a campus in Saigon or an exhausting day drilling a well in a Ugandan village. It is the ongoing rub of life against life, multiple conversations, myriad demonstrations of the kingdom. It's easy to return from a short-term mission trip with a handful of exciting stories of how God has been at work. But real mission—the ordinary kind to which we're all called every day—is not so neat, and the stories don't all have happy endings. When we follow Jesus' example, we enter a lifelong journey with the poor, the lost, the unbelieving, the hostile. When we follow Jesus' example, we realize that incarnational mission invites us into the messiness, the chaos, and the sadness of people's lives, not just the occasional great moments of breakthrough.

To follow Jesus' incarnational example is to take seriously his message and his modeling that we are sent into a broken, unruly world, in which his reign is not fully understood nor acknowledged. We are sent as his agents of shalom in a world of anger and violence. He even commissions his disciples to go out like lambs among wolves. He knows that the missional call involves a decision to participate in the unfurling of his kingdom of peace in the face of a broken world of anger and violence. This is clear in his teaching as well as in the example of his life. It finds particular focus in his references to himself as the good shepherd. When Jesus identifies himself as a shepherd, he does so knowing that he is drawing on a wealth of Old Testament imagery, where such a metaphor is applied most consistently to Yahweh or King David. Jesus is self-consciously identifying with both the Father and his descendant (and antecedent), David. Take, for example, Psalm 28, which in part reads:

> The LORD is the strength of his people,
>   a fortress of salvation for his anointed one.
> Save your people and bless your inheritance;
>   *be their shepherd* and carry them forever. (vv. 8–9, italics added)

And similarly, Psalm 80 refers to the shepherding role of Yahweh:

> Hear us, O Shepherd of Israel,
>   you who lead Joseph like a flock;
> you who sit enthroned between the cherubim, shine forth
>   (v. 1)

And in one of the most beautiful passages in Isaiah, the tenderness of Yahweh's shepherding role with Israel is juxtaposed with his awesome majesty as the one, true and only God:

He [the LORD] tends his flock like a shepherd:
  He gathers the lambs in his arms
and carries them close to his heart;
  he gently leads those that have young.
Who has measured the waters in the hollow of his hand,
  or with the breadth of his hand marked off the heavens?
Who has held the dust of the earth in a basket,
  or weighed the mountains on the scales
  and the hills in a balance? (Isa. 40:11–12)

Of course, the best known example of Yahweh's role as the good shepherd occurs in the much-loved and oft-quoted Twenty-Third Psalm, beginning as it does, "The LORD is my shepherd . . ." But my point is that Psalm 23 is not an isolated instance, and this is not to mention the various passages that describe David as the nation's shepherd. It was a well-known allusion and one that was held dear by the people of Israel. It indicated that God held them close, remained devoted to them, and was ever-reliant, always vigilant to their needs.

So when Jesus appropriates this symbol for himself, he is saying something very clear about his role in the life of Israel and his status as the Messiah. He is Yahweh's presence on earth. He is the fulfillment of all of Israel's Davidic hope. He reveals to Israel what it looks like when God draws near—indeed, when God moves into the neighborhood. All his references to the role of the shepherd in John 10 reveal elements of incarnational mission—compassion, closeness, vigilance, loyalty, devotion. But he recasts that role in a stark and shocking way when he says, "I am the good shepherd. The good shepherd *lays down his life for the sheep*" (John 10:11, italics added). By adopting this reference to himself, and then telling us that a shepherd sacrifices himself for the sheep, he is telling us about the way of mission. As mentioned earlier, when mission is patterned on the life of Jesus, it must include sacrifice, including solidarity with the poor, vulnerable love, and a risky challenge to the status quo. We cannot claim the right to shepherd the people of our neighborhoods unless we're equally willing to lay down our lives, to embrace sacrifice and service for them. Too many preachers want to make pronouncements or throw their ecclesial weight around, demanding they be listened to, or that their neighbors acknowledge them as shepherds or pastors in their village. Incarnational mission, modeled on Jesus' example, must have a dimension of selfless sacrifice for it to be considered genuinely incarnational.

The Participation in Christ (Passion)

To be incarnational also means to place an emphasis on the continuing presence and initiative of the risen Christ, without which discipleship and mission is impossible. Jesus is alive and his reign is apparent not just in the grand sweep of history but in the hearts and minds of the redeemed. In this respect, to participate in Christ is to share his passion, a much-abused term these days. People will tell you they are passionate about all sorts of things, but the term actually comes from the Latin *passiō*, derived from the verb meaning to suffer or to endure. Passion is more than having a strong feeling about a person or thing. It is the intense and compelling enthusiasm for something for which you are willing to suffer. Incarnationally, this means that missional Christians should be filled with the passion of Christ, filled with a deep enthusiasm for the cause to which he has called them. It is Christ in us, the hope of glory, that fills us with energy and vigor for the missional cause.

It seems to me that this goes a long way toward helping us to not see mission as begrudging, resentful obedience to the command of Jesus. Rather it is a creative calling to participate in Jesus' passion. Mother Teresa was noted for having said, "Give yourself fully to God. He will use you to accomplish great things on the condition that you believe much more in His love than in your own weakness."[9] Too often well-meaning missionaries have used the so-called Great Commission to motivate Christians to serve missionally, demanding that because Jesus barked the order "Go into all the world" that we are disobedient foot soldiers if we resist him. But Jesus' words in Matthew 28 shouldn't be characterized as an order from our sergeant-major. Instead they are a dynamic and creative summary of all the disciples have seen and lived, couched as an invitation to take them wherever the disciples might go, even to the end of the world and to the end of the age. They have, to use Mother Teresa's words, given themselves fully to God, coming under his reign through Jesus. Like them, we are similarly commissioned to live fully under God's reign and to serve him and his world freely as one filled with the passion of the suffering Savior.

Joining in God's Incarnational Mission (Prevenience)

The third dimension of incarnational mission addressed by missiologist Ross Langmead is that of joining God's ongoing mission in the world. That involves a commitment to continually reach out as God does, to partner with him in the unfurling of his kingdom. It assumes the prevenient grace of God. That is, it assumes that God is already at work in our world—that being incarnational means stepping into what God is doing and remaining faithful to that calling. The missio Dei is not a short-term project. God is at work, bringing to completion all he began in the act of creation. To join him in that task is to seek to discover what God is doing in our sphere of influence and attention and submitting ourselves to it.

That might mean moving into a new neighborhood across town, as Nigel Barham calls people to do. It might mean crossing the seas to move into a new neighborhood elsewhere in the world, as Kenneth Bailey did. Or it might mean entering more intentionally into God's work and presence in the neighborhoods in which we already live. Whatever the sphere of influence and attention, we need to be fully present to what God is doing there and join him over the long haul.

Many will be familiar with the extraordinary work done by British missionary Jackie Pullinger in Hong Kong. In 1966, Pullinger embarked on a French ship sailing from Europe to the Far East. The ship stopped at a number of ports, and at each one the young would-be missionary, with no mission agency backing or any specific ministry plan, simply prayed that God would direct her when to disembark. His answer came when the ship pulled into Hong Kong. She eventually found her way to Kowloon's notorious Walled City, called the City of Darkness by locals because it was a hotbed of triad gang activity, opium dens, crime, death, and despair. Jackie Pullinger moved into the Walled City and began what is now over forty years of faithful incarnational service, beginning with a youth club, summer camps, remedial learning classes, and leading to what is today named the St. Stephen's Society, a fully fledged charitable agency for alleviating suffering and preaching the gospel in Hong Kong. In the late 1990s the Walled City was demolished by the Hong Kong authorities in an attempt to clean up the city. But Jackie Pullinger remained, resolute in her devotion to the neighborhood to which God sent her. To hear Pullinger speak today about sharing a room with three other Chinese women, or facing down drug dealers and gangsters, or having no food to offer a starving teenager, or driving demons out of drug addicts is a remarkable experience, not only because of the tales of high adventure she often tells, but because of the gravitas that comes with her doing so for over four decades.

Compare this with Ken Bailey's forty years in the Middle East, or Mother Teresa's over forty-five years of ministering to the poor, sick, orphaned, and dying of Calcutta. These examples serve to remind us that God's mission is long term, and that when joining God in incarnational service, we must assume it will likewise be a lengthy tenure, if not a lifelong one.

Such a yearning for the incarnational presence of God in our midst appears in works of great literature from time to time. I think of Willa Cather's *Death Comes for the Archbishop*, a brilliant evocation of Catholic mission in the Arizona territories at the turn of the twentieth century, and Georges Bernanos' French classic *Diary of a Country Priest*. But nowhere have I seen it more powerfully presented than in the 2006 Pulitzer Prize–winning novel *Gilead* by Marilynne Robinson. Set in mid-1950s Iowa and narrated by Rev. John Ames, an aging minister in failing health, *Gilead* is written in the form of a long letter meant for the seven-year-old son born of his much younger second wife, a gift (and confession) to be read after the death of a father who won't be around to see his boy grow up. Slowly and graciously, Ames tells of his family history, including both his father and grandfather who were also ministers in Gilead, and by so doing he describes the regrets and the pleasures, the reminiscences and religious reflections, and the acute observations of the natural world that make up his lifelong service of the town. Ames's letter contains precise evocations of a minister's daily life, the everydayness and the frequent banality of holy life. He complains about a "molded salad of orange gelatin with stuffed green olives and shredded cabbage and anchovies that has dogged my ministerial life," and finds that a certain bean dish looks "distinctly Presbyterian." He reflects on the thousands of sermons he has written for his parish over the years, all of them filed in boxes in his attic. Now, at seventy-six, he tries to calculate their value in the light of their impending destruction after his death:

> Say, fifty sermons a year for forty-five years, not counting funerals and so on, of which there have been a great many. . . . Say three hundred pages make a volume. Then I've written two hundred twenty-five books, which puts me up there with Augustine and Calvin for quantity. . . . I wrote almost all of it in the deepest hope and conviction. . . . Trying to say what was true. . . . It's humiliating to have written as much as Augustine, and then to have to find a way to dispose of it.[10]

Gilead is an almost otherworldly book, written with such authenticity in the modestly magnificent voice of Rev. John Ames, a man who it seems never even considered abandoning the good folk of Gilead nor his vocation, as one who would lay down his life for his sheep. All those filed sermons are testimony to the ordinary wonder of everyday service and long-term commitment. In a day and age when ministers rush from one appointment to the next, always looking for so-called better opportunities, always seeking to move into greater influence, John Ames's letter is in stark contrast. As is the life and work of Bailey, Pullinger, and Mother Teresa. It seems to me that joining in God's mission involves not just a few special moments of missional effectiveness, not simply a handful of dramatic anecdotes, but boxes and boxes of filed sermons, prayers, exorcisms, meals, spare beds, conversations, rebukes, confessions, encouragements, and appeals.

The other thing I need to say about joining God's incarnational mission is that biblically it can be demonstrated that God has a peculiar bias toward the poor and the marginalized. Not only should we embrace a long-term view on mission, but we need to ask about where God is already at work, and in every likelihood that will be among the disenfranchised. To ignore this dimension of the missio Dei is to miss a defining quality of biblical mission. As I've already mentioned, when looking for traces of the kingdom in the neighborhood to which we've been sent, demonstrations of social justice should be on our radar. Too many not-yet-missional churches are happy to fall into the trap of assuming the commuter church model and the prosperity gospel are normal and acceptable expressions of Christian mission without realizing how much they play into the deterioration of our neighborhoods. In stark contrast to this, John Perkins advocates an incarnational approach, where

> churches that maintain a vital presence in a community, and those who abandon their upwardly mobile ways to identify with others less fortunate than they are, preserve society and guard against the deterioration of local communities across America. The evangelical church has to recreate family and community by becoming an incarnate presence in society rather than remaining transient and self-consumed, by proclaiming the gospel of reconciliation rather than the gospel reduced to church growth and success. If we truly incarnate the church in a community, then we are better able to participate in God's redemption of the poor from oppression and act out divine jubilee justice.[11]

Indeed, the withdrawal by the church from neighborhoods— whether physical and literal or simply relational—only reinforces the very social trends that Christians find abhorrent. But as Dr. Perkins says, a truly incarnated church joins God's mission in the redemption of the poor and the institution of godly justice, which leads to renewed neighborhoods. This might take a variety of forms, but a few that readily come to mind include

- *Community Building*—This means considering how we and our neighbors might live together to support one another. In many instances it will be the followers of Jesus who broker neighborhood discussions about ways they can work on being intentional in their life together. The co-housing movement is a great example of one of the outcomes of this kind of discussion.
- *Voluntary Simplicity*—Surely, the incarnational Christian community can model how our lifestyles affect one another and our world, and how we can free up resources to address the needs of others.

- *Sustainable Business*—Again, why can't the church stimulate ways we as a neighborhood can consider sustainable and ethical work practices in local businesses (as well as in our churches) and how we can work together to provide opportunities for others. Worker co-ops are a great example.
- *Buy Local*—An incarnational church would have to see the support of local businesses and the purchase of fair trade products as an essential, particularly to encourage a sound local economy.
- *Holistic Wellness*—An incarnational church, drawn as it is into the everyday difficulties of its neighbors, would naturally be inclined to commit to supporting one another in physical, emotional, spiritual, and relational health.

These are just examples of how we can flesh out loving our neighbors and integrating our politics, spirituality, and mission in our lifestyle, linking with the prevenient grace of God, who is at work in our neighborhoods. If we take Jesus' example for incarnational mission seriously, and if we're filled and renewed by the presence of the living Christ, and if we remain committed to long-term mission in our neighborhoods, including among the poor and marginalized, I believe we have moved much closer to a truly missional framework.

Where Is Jesus in Your Neighborhood?

Christine Sine, from Mustard Seed Associates in Seattle, recently posted the following observation on her blog:

> Yesterday as I was driving to a local church to speak, I passed a homeless man standing on the street corner. That was not unusual. The corner he stood at was a popular place for the destitute to beg. His face was hidden by a sign that read *Homeless and Hungry*. That wasn't unusual either. As the impact of the recession continues, more people are being driven onto the streets to live. What was unusual was that the sign was written in seven different languages.[12]

You or I might think of that as merely quirky or even charming. It never ceases to amaze me how clever some of the cardboard signs held by homeless people can be ("Ninjas killed my family—need money for kung fu lessons"; "Wife has been kidnapped—I'm 98¢ short for ransom"). But Christine's observation on the multilingual sign she saw was insightful. Commenting on the resourcefulness of the homeless, she pointed out that clearly the man with the sign knew that there were at least seven different language groups present in that neighborhood: "This man obviously knows the neighborhood far better than I do. He knows who lives in the area and how to communicate with them." On the other hand, she believed the traditional church she was visiting that day was far less savvy about their neighbors:

> Not only were they unaware of the man that stood on the corner only a few hundred yards from their door, they were also unaware of the rich ethnic diversity that surrounded them and certainly had little desire to reach out and encounter that diversity. Not surprisingly this church was shrinking. And the parishioners were withdrawing in fear and denial, talking about removing the last row of pews so that the seats did not look so empty. We live in a strange world when the homeless are better acquainted with their world and can respond better to changes and transitions than the church does.[13]

Truly incarnational Christians live in the neighborhoods where they're serving God. They are deeply concerned about partnering with the unfurling of God's kingdom so they do know who lives there and what cultural and social expressions are present. They take the idea of place very seriously. I've heard it said that place is just a space that has a narrative history. The job of the missional community is to learn that history and to retell it in a redemptive way. The panhandler with the multilingual sign has learned the history of his place, but he is not retelling it redemptively. He is using it for his own ends, and who can blame him? It is our job as the followers of Jesus to invite people into the new history that God is writing, to show them that the reign of God is unfurling across the world and throughout history, and to invite others to make that story their story. If we don't even know what has been and is currently happening in our neighborhood, how can we retell the story with a view to the future God has in store? I recall seeing the front page of a small paper in north Seattle that read "How local is local when it comes to your food?" This got me thinking: How local is local when it comes to your church?

During the first half of 2010, my wife and I took an extended sabbatical together and lived in the Echo Park area of Los Angeles. While there, we discovered a local café that really had the neighborhood's interests at heart. Masa of Echo Park is located at 1800 West Sunset. In the early 1900s their building was a Model T car dealership when Echo Park was the center of the film business. Now it's a very cool bakery and café, committed to community activism, environmental sustainability, and excellent deep dish pizza. They heavily promote a local after-school teen mentoring program. They'll also give you a 50 percent discount on any meal if you adopt a homeless animal from the nearby Echo Park Animal Alliance. They put on a neighborhood pizza party every time the Dodgers play at their nearby stadium. They open their space up for local groups doing fundraisers for worthy charities. All their take-out packaging is biodegradable. Even the wine corks are recycled—turned into art by a local craftsman. Every time we ate there, we would read the newsletter they place on every table. It not only promoted events held in their restaurant, but other community events (the annual blessing of the bicycles by the Society of St. Vincent de Paul, volunteer drives by various groups), as well as showcasing other businesses in town (including other cafés) and welcoming all new businesses into the neighborhood. Their attitude was so, well, Christian, we wondered whether Masa was managed by Christians. Then, between mouthfuls of pizza, we were reading the newsletter one day and we came across an article paying tribute to a local saint, one who had helped Masa when it was getting started. Though lengthy, it is a great example of an incarnational witness by an amazing woman who loves her neighborhood as Jesus does:

> Everyone loves Miss Judy! Spend any time in Echo Park and you know one of the great ambassadors of the community, Judy. Judy grew up in Dallas, but moved to Los Angeles in the early 70s on a mission—literally!—to attend Missionary School. How does a small town girl get up the gumption to pick and move to the big city on her own? Why inspiration, of course, in the form of a plan to read Bible verses to Cary Grant over the phone (hey, she got through to his agent). She

had intended to travel the world doing missionary work, but after meeting so many people in need right here in the neighborhood, she decided to stay put. To this day she works tirelessly for the church (our neighbor, the Angelus Temple) caretaking for those in need—and is just a red-haired beam of sunshine to everyone around the neighborhood. Around 2004, Judy and her pal, Tom, walked into Masa on our opening day, and decided that like with everyone else she meets she'd take us under her wing. Masa's success is in no small part due to Tom and Judy. Seriously! They were so determined to see us get through that notoriously tough first year, and they came every single day, sometimes three times a day! They were an immediate fit with the kind of homey, fun, inclusive place we wanted Masa to be, and became an emotional support-system-duo to everyone here. Not only that, Judy is a one-woman PR machine! Every time she was here—or anywhere for that matter—she got busy spreading the word about Masa (not dissimilar to her missionary work)! I can't tell you how many times she struck up a conversation about the bread pudding or the burgers or how great Masa was to anyone and everyone. Before we had much staff at all, Judy even jumped in to help (she wouldn't even let us buy her a meal, and we fought hard!). There's no denying the power of Judy. We love you, Judy![14]

Here is the example of a missional Christian who has made the sacrificial decision to move into her neighborhood, looking for traces of the kingdom wherever she might find them. In Masa she discovered a business that was committed to such kingdom values as ecological sustainability, justice, peace, and beauty, and she brought to bear her not inconsiderable energies on supporting what Jesus was doing there. And she is loved by the neighborhood for doing so. How might we better incarnate in our neighborhoods? How can we learn and retell the narrative history of our place, finding the redemptive threads in that story? In his book *Borderland Churches*, Canadian church leader Gary Nelson suggests a number of simple steps for getting to know where Jesus is in our neighborhoods. They include

- *Attend special community activities,* such as youth events, ball games, garage sales, political events, community organization meetings;

- *Investigate both the official and common names of your neighborhood*, recognizing that sometimes communities have nicknames or reputations beyond their official name, and ask whether these perceptions are fair and accurate;
- *Walk, drive, and ride your neighborhood* during three distinct periods of the day—morning, early evening, and late evening—including traveling the public transportation system to discover who lives there and where they go;
- *Observe what kinds of buildings* are in your neighborhood, including churches, schools, commercial spaces, art galleries, community spaces, and in what ways they contribute to the shape of the neighborhood—for example, is there gentrification or deterioration in your community?;
- *Observe where the social gathering areas are*—bars, clubs, parks, malls, etc.—noting what kind of spaces they are and who frequents them;
- *Meet the social service providers* in your community and ask them who they serve and what their greatest challenges are.[15]

Essentially, Nelson is trying to engage churches in an interest in discovering what traces of the reign of God the people in their neighborhoods are detecting. He is calling the not-yet-missional to move in, to listen, to care, to incarnate the gospel in those places. This requires enormous energy and selfless resolve, but it is an effort worth making. We need to stop driving through our neighborhood on our way to church. We need a movement of incarnational missional Christians willing to serve their neighbors and to alert them to the universal reign of God through Christ. As Alan Roxburgh so beautifully puts it,

We need a movement of God's people into neighborhoods, to live out and be the new future of Christ. It must be a movement that demonstrates how the people of God have a vision and the power to transform our world. This is not the same as current attempts to grow bigger and bigger churches that act like vacuum cleaners, sucking people out of their neighborhoods into a sort of Christian supermarket. Our culture does not need any more churches run like corporations; it needs local communities empowered by the gospel vision of a transforming Christ who addresses the needs of the context and changes the polis into a place of hope and wholeness. The corporation churches we are cloning across the land cannot birth this transformational vision, because they have no investment in context or place; they are centers of expressive individualism with a truncated gospel of personal salvation and little else. Our penchant for bigness and numerical success as the sign of God's blessing only discourages and deflects attempts to root communities of God's people deeply into neighborhoods. And until we build transformed communities there is no hope for a broken earth.[16]

CONCLUSION

The Sound of Worlds Colliding

In his book *The Sound of Worlds Colliding*, missionary to Cambodia's urban poor Kristin Jack tells the tragically comical story of how one of his co-workers once impersonated the American ambassador in order to unfreeze aid to the victims of fires that had raged across the slums of Phnom Penh.

Jack himself lived in the riverside slum of Chbaa Ampou, and when part of it went up in flames, he had to stand by helplessly and watch over 900 homes be destroyed, leaving almost 6,000 people homeless. Many had escaped the flames by throwing themselves into the nearby Bassac River. The homeless survivors were relocated to abandoned rice paddies twenty-five kilometers from the city, where they were dumped with no shelter, no infrastructure, and no amenities. Their plight was desperate. These people had lost everything—possessions, savings, even their meager food stores. Quickly, NGOs and churches rallied, assembling emergency food supplies and household goods for the victims. All was ready for the mobilization of the emergency supplies when an astonishing edict came from the government. No aid was to be distributed. The people were deemed squatters, illegally using public land, and no assistance was to be permitted.

Kristin Jack and his colleagues then entered into tense negotiations with local military commanders and government officials, urging them to reconsider, begging for the lives of the poor. But it was all to no avail. The military wouldn't budge. Jack tells what happened next:

> Just when it seemed we were totally stale-mated, and that all of our careful planning was about to fail, a shiny blue car pulled up . . . and out stepped our friend, Rick Drummond, dressed in a dark blue suit and tie for a church service he was to lead later that morning. A tall, dignified man in his 60s, Rick was an elder statesman-missionary, . . . now mentor and guide to an ethnic Vietnamese church in Chbaa Ampou, one of the churches participating with us in the emergency aid distribution effort. Rick had come to check how things were progressing.[1]

Dressed in this manner and with his dignified bearing, Rick the missionary was mistaken by the Cambodian officials as an American diplomat. Rumors began circulating around the gathering of military commanders and government personnel, but because Rick was fluent in Vietnamese, not Khmer, he didn't understand what they were saying. But Jack, a longtime resident of Cambodia, knew exactly what was happening. He continues:

> I heard the soldiers in the background talking nervously, speculating that this new arrival was the American ambassador. Suppressing a smile, I glanced in their direction and nodded. Quickly the rumor spread around the circle: this man in the suit was in fact the Ambassador of the United States of America! Rick . . . could see he had become the center of attention and that his presence was causing quite a stir, but he had no idea why. "Kristin, what are they saying—what's going on?"
>
> "I'll tell you later. Just look serious and keep nodding your head."[2]

Without confirming nor denying their misunderstanding, and leaving Rick completely unaware of the subterfuge, Jack watched the Cambodian officials become more and more agitated about upsetting the US consulate. Soon, they agreed to allow the aid to be delivered, telling Jack that they had decided to be generous in this instance, all the while keeping eye contact with the "American ambassador," who just kept looking serious and nodding his head.

We do live under the sound of worlds colliding. There's the world of slums and fires, destruction and poverty, government inaction and corruption. And there's the world of generosity, love, compassion, beauty, and justice. There's the earth as we find it, and there's the kingdom of heaven. And because of the incarnation, the death, and the resurrection of Jesus, the latter world has come crashing into the former world. Heaven has come to earth, even if we can only perceive its presence fitfully, partially, and mysteriously. It is here, invading the earth with purpose, unfurling itself across broken human societies everywhere. And in the middle of these colliding worlds we, the missional ones, stand like ambassadors, delegates from one world to the other, alerting people to the reign of God through Christ, representing the world as it is waiting to be reborn. Kristin Jack's story epitomizes our calling as ambassadors, to nod and keep smiling and to remain in service to the missio Dei, representing God in and over against the world in "a ceaseless celebration of the Feast of the Epiphany."[3]

When we are being effective missional ambassadors from one world to another, we are looking to see transformation—both the transformation of neighborhoods and the transformation of individuals. If God's universal reign is acknowledged and cooperated with, we ought to see less injustice, less poverty, less hatred in our neighborhoods. We also ought to see less unbelief. When we alert people to God's rule, we do so by inviting people to place their unbelief under that rule. We invite people to acknowledge God's reign and to bend their knee to his rule in their lives. This results in dramatic and meaningful personal transformation. It opens us to the experience of grace, of God's relentless and unearned love and mercy. And it invites us to become agents of that grace, ambassadors of a whole new world order, one based on grace, not fear or greed. But further, as graced ones we have our eyes opened to the beauty of God's reign and its signs in art, music, food, literature, architecture, and nature. We crave beauty—not the unredeemed Hollywood version or the repulsive, manipulative version of pornography, but the redeemed godly versions we find in breathtaking vistas, in refracted light and dollops of paint, in delicious cuisine and beautiful buildings, in soaring tunes and majestic canvases. But I stress again this is an appreciation of true beauty that doesn't limit the beautiful things of life to the trinkets and baubles of consumer culture. As Kristin Jack says, "We must ask God to give us the eyes to see his beauty buried everywhere, even in pain and poverty, even among those crippled with disease and approaching death."[4]

As such delegates from one world to the next, we must also create foretastes (film trailers, as I mentioned at the beginning of this book) of the joy and freedom and sense of celebration that exist in the world which is here and coming, the world of God's reign through Jesus. Every Sunday night the community to which I belong meets for a big meal together. We gather around low feasting tables and enjoy great food and conversation. We accept all comers, offering them a meal and wine and a seat at our table. We share our joys, our doubts, and our fears. We celebrate our freedom and speak openly of our allegiance to the lordship of Jesus in the breaking of bread and the drinking of wine, symbolizing his supreme sacrifice and his death and resurrection as the ultimate shaper of our lives, both individual and together. Children run amok. Music is played. Laughter comes in bursts. The Bible is read and explained. We gather together in a spirit of celebration because we believe we have been rescued from one world which is fading into a new world that is unfurling, a world of laughter and bread and music and fellowship and inclusion and freedom. I believe that celebration is a core practice of those who live in a world under God's reign, but I'm not sure whether a rip-roaring "contemporary worship service" is going to quite do it. I'd prefer a celebration similar to that which Nehemiah commends: "Go and enjoy choice food and sweet drinks, and send some to those who have nothing prepared. This day is sacred to our Lord. Do not grieve, for the joy of the LORD is your strength" (Neh. 8:10). Celebration, beauty, and generosity are a godly combination.

Or similarly in Zechariah 8, the prophet sketches Yahweh's promises to Jerusalem with images of celebration, satisfaction, and joy. He describes old men and women sitting contentedly on the streets of the city as children play innocently around them (vv. 4–5) and of workers earning a fair wage for their efforts (v. 10) and of the earth yielding a bountiful harvest (v. 12). He calls the people to embrace "seasons of joy and gladness" and to "love truth and peace" (v. 19 NRSV). He sings up a new song about a new world, a world of justice and plenty, peace and grace. And he dreams of a day when such a world will be desired more than the trappings and misfortunes of the other world that is fading away. His song is so beautiful, he is such a brilliant ambassador for this new world, that he even imagines a stampede of people knocking down every obstacle to enter into this city. He writes,

> And many peoples and powerful nations will come to Jerusalem to seek the LORD Almighty and to entreat him. This is what the LORD Almighty says: "In those days ten men from all languages and nations will take firm hold of one Jew by the hem of his robe and say, 'Let us go with you, because we have heard that God is with you.'" (Zech. 8:22–23)

I dare to believe that if the church in the West can rediscover and embrace its mandate to fashion trailers of the world that is to come, we too would be beset by others from every language and nation, begging us to bring them under God's reign through Christ because they have heard that God is with us.

And yet, like the phony American "ambassador" in Kristin Jack's story, we are equally unqualified for this task. We are poor reflections of the king we represent. We are inadequate representatives of his reign and the world he is ushering into existence. And yet, somehow, for some reason, God chooses to use us, often in spite of our ignorance or our limitations. I love the image of Rick Drummond innocently waving to the draconian Khmer commanders, blissfully unaware of the drama playing out around him. It reminds me of the hilarious band of absconding penguins in the animated film *Madagascar*. Whenever they find themselves in a spot and have to bluff their way out, the lead penguin, speaking with the menacing drawl of a New York mobster, says to his associates, "Smile and wave, boys, just smile and wave." I'm sure I don't know the half of what God is doing in and through me. I'm a poor version of an ambassador, but I often find myself representing him in the strangest situations, and I too just smile and wave, trusting in the unstoppable nature of God's reign and the wisdom of his grace and favor, as I hear the sound of worlds colliding all around me.

And so I'm still using the M-word, despite the fact that some people tell me how passé it is. But I'm using it steadfastly and resolutely to describe the wholesale and thorough reorientation of the church around mission, a mission that includes evangelism, but more: a mission that is anchored in the task of alerting people to the rule of God through Christ and which can never be reduced to the recruitment of new attendees at our meetings; a mission that hopes in the ongoing work of God to redeem all things and set everything right in accordance with his will; a mission that by its very nature must be lived out incarnationally, in close proximity to those to whom we've been sent; a mission that is cross-shaped and calls its followers to the disciplines of sacrifice, service, love, and grace; and a mission that delights in beauty, flavor, joy, and friendship, that lifts us up and fills us with the same fullness of life we see in Jesus.

NOTES

Introduction

1. Michael Frost and Alan Hirsch, *The Shaping of Things to Come* (Peabody, MA: Hendrickson, 2003), ix.

2. Quoted in Ed Stetzer, *Planting Missional Churches* (Nashville: Broadman & Holman, 2006), 13.

3. *USA Today*, February 17, 2010, http://www.usatoday.com/news/religion/2010-02-17-pewyouth17_ST_N.html (cited April 3, 2010).

4. Ed Stetzer, Rich Stanley, and Jason Hayne, *Lost and Found: The Younger Unchurched and the Churches That Reach Them* (Nashville: Broadman and Holman, 2009), 44.

5. Ibid.

6. Ibid., 43.

7. Reggie McNeal, *Missional Renaissance: Changing the Scoreboard for the Church* (San Francisco: Jossey-Bass, 2009), 179.

8. Jesse Bogan, "America's Biggest Megachurches," *Forbes.com*, June 26, 2009, http://www.forbes.com/2009/06/26/americas-biggest-megachurches-business-megachurches.html.

9. McNeal, *Missional Renaissance*, xiv.

10. Clint Rainey, "Mega Burnout," *Dallas Morning News*, Saturday, July 23, 2005, 29A.

11. Ibid.

12. Neil Cole, *Church 3.0: Upgrades for the Future of the Church* (San Francisco: Jossey-Bass, 2010), 29.

Chapter 1 The Missio Dei

1. David Bosch, *Believing in the Future: Toward a Missiology of Western Culture* (Valley Forge, PA: Trinity Press, 1995), 33.

2. David Bosch, *Witness to the World: The Christian Mission in Theological Perspective* (Atlanta: John Knox Press, 1980), 18.

3. David Bosch, *Transforming Mission: Paradigm Shifts in Theology of Mission* (Maryknoll, NY: Orbis, 1991), 519.

4. Lesslie Newbigin, *The Open Secret: An Introduction to the Theology of Mission,* rev. ed. (Grand Rapids: Eerdmans, rev. ed. 1995), 33–34.

5. N. T. Wright, *Simply Christian: Why Christianity Makes Sense* (New York: Harper-Collins, 2006), 217.

6. Thomas Torrance, *The Christian Frame of Mind: Reason, Order, and Openness in Theology and Natural Science* (Colorado Springs: Helmers & Howard, 1989), 21.

7. Summarized from Bosch, *Transforming Mission*, 409–20.

8. See John Stott, *Christian Mission in the Modern World* (Downers Grove, IL: Inter-Varsity Press, 1976), 35ff.

9. Lesslie Newbigin, *Missionary Theologian: A Reader*, ed. Paul Weston (London: SPCK, 2006), 264.

10. Bosch, *Transforming Mission*, 391.

11. Ibid.

12. Tim Keller, quoted from session he delivered at the Reform and Resurge Conference in May 2006. Posted at http://theresurgence.com/2006/07/18/doing-justice-audio (cited May 5, 2010).

13. Torrance, *Christian Frame of Mind*, 21.

14. Scot McKnight, *Embracing Grace: A Gospel for All of Us* (Brewster, MA: Paraclete Press, 2005), 12.

15. Lois Barrett, ed., *Treasure in Clay Jars: Patterns in Missional Faithfulness* (Grand Rapids: Eerdmans, 2004), x.

Chapter 2 Slow Evangelism

1. Brian McLaren, *More Ready Than You Realize: Evangelism as Dance in the Postmodern Matrix* (Grand Rapids: Zondervan, 2002), back cover.

2. Dan Kimball, *The Emerging Church: Vintage Christianity for New Generations* (Grand Rapids: Zondervan, 2003), 197–211.

3. Frost and Hirsch, *Shaping of Things to Come*, 53–59.

4. Mark Driscoll, "A Pastoral Perspective on the Emergent Church," *Criswell Theological Review* 3, no. 2 (March 27, 2006): 90.

5. I am referring here to the controversy regarding Steve Chalke's book, *The Lost Message of Jesus* (Grand Rapids: Zondervan, 2003), which was critiqued in Don Carson's *Becoming Conversant with the Emerging Church* (Grand Rapids: Zondervan, 2005), and which touched off a significant debate about the validity of a penal substitutionary view of the atonement.

6. David Bosch, quoted in Stan Nussbaum, *A Reader's Guide to Transforming Mission* (Maryknoll, NY: Orbis Books, 2005), 105.

7. Slow Food website: http://www.slowfood.com/ (cited March 20, 2010).

8. Bryan Stone, *Evangelism after Christendom: The Theology and Practice of Christian Witness* (Grand Rapids: Brazos, 2007), 316.

9. Bosch, *Transforming Mission*, 420.

10. Bosch, quoted in Nussbaum, *Reader's Guide*, 107.

11. James Choung, *True Story: A Christianity Worth Believing In* (Downers Grove, IL: InterVarsity, 2008).

12. David Benson's booklet, *Epic Story*, is an unpublished resource of Kenmore Baptist Church, Brisbane. For further information, see http://pathways.kbc.org.au/passing-it-on/.

13. Peter Stuhlmacher, *Paul's Letter to the Romans*, trans. S. Hafemann (Louisville: Westminster/John Knox Press, 1994), 19.

14. Susan Hope, *Mission-Shaped Spirituality: The Transforming Power of Mission* (London: Church House Publishing, 2007), 75.

15. Stanley Hauerwas and William Willimon, *Resident Aliens: Life in the Christian Colony* (Nashville: Abingdon, 1989), 94.

16. Ralph Waldo Emerson, quoted in George Hunter, *The Celtic Way of Evangelism* (Nashville: Abingdon, 2000), 57.

17. Bosch, *Transforming Mission*, 33.

18. Lesslie Newbigin, *The Household of God* (London: SCM Press, 1964), 140.

19. C. René Padilla, *Mission Between the Times: Essays on the Kingdom* (Grand Rapids: Eerdmans, 1985), 22.

20. Hope, *Mission-Shaped Spirituality*, 93.

21. Soong-Chan Rah, *The Next Evangelicalism: Freeing the Church from Western Cultural Captivity* (Downers Grove, IL: InterVarsity, 2009), 167.

22. Ibid., 177.

23. Stephen Beaven, "A Christian Initiative at a Gresham Apartment Complex Bears Fruit," *The Oregonian*, August 27, 2010, http://www.oregonlive.com/gresham/index.ssf/2010/08/a_christian_initiative_at_a_gr.html.

Chapter 3 A Market-Shaped Church

1. "Easter Eggs and More Than $1M in Prizes at S. Texas Megachurch," *Caller.com*, March 27, 2010, http://www.caller.com/news/2010/mar/27/the-million-dollar-giveaway/ (cited March 29, 2010).

2. Bosch, quoted in Nussbaum, *Reader's Guide*, 105.

3. "Easter Eggs," *Caller.com*.

4. Stone, *Evangelism after Christendom*, 315.

5. This very point is made by Dan Kimball in his book, *They Like Jesus but Not the Church: Insights from Emerging Generations* (Grand Rapids: Zondervan, 2007), based on his research among young adults in northern California.

6. Laurie Goldstein, "Evangelicals Fear the Loss of Their Teenagers," *New York Times*, October 6, 2006, http://www.nytimes.com/2006/10/06/us/06evangelical.

7. Ibid.

8. G. Jeffrey MacDonald, "Congregations Gone Wild," *New York Times*, August 8, 2010, WK9, http://www.nytimes.com/2010/08/08/opinion/08macdonald.html.

9. Walter Brueggemann, *The Prophetic Imagination* (Minneapolis: Augsburg Fortress, 2001), 1.

10. Skye Jethani, *The Divine Commodity: Discovering a Faith beyond Consumer Christianity* (Grand Rapids: Zondervan, 2009), 50.

11. Ibid., 111–12.

12. Ted Olsen, "Buffy's Religion," *Christianity Today* online, posted 7/08/2002, http://www.christianitytoday.com/ct/2002/008/36.10.html.

13. MacDonald, "Congregations Gone Wild," WK9.

14. Ibid.

15. Stone, *Evangelism after Christendom*, 49.

16. Ross Gittins, *Business Day*, "What Would Jesus Do about Economic Growth?" *Sydney Morning Herald*, June 14, 2010, 8–9, http://www.smh.com.au/business/what-would-jesus-do-about-economic-growth-20100613-y61b.html.

17. Ibid.

18. Lesslie Newbigin, *The Other Side of 1984: Questions for the Churches* (Geneva: World Council of Churches, 1983), 40.

19. David E. Fitch, *The Great Giveaway: Reclaiming the Mission of the Church from Big Business* (Grand Rapids: Baker, 2005), 229.

20. This is my summary of the general points made by Fitch, p. 229.

21. Jeff Israeli and Howard Chua-Eoan, "The Trial of Benedict XVI," *Time*, June 7, 2010, 43.

22. Howard Snyder, *Liberating the Church: The Ecology of Church and Kingdom* (Eugene, OR: Wipf and Stock, 1996), 11.

Chapter 4 Triumphant Humiliation

1. All the following quotes from Enter the Kingdom come from "Heckled Christian band know how Jesus felt," *The Onion*, May 17, 2010, http://www.theonion.com/articles/heckled-christian-rock-band-knows-how-jesus-felt,17446/ (cited May 20, 2010).

2. Alan Hirsch and Debra Hirsch, *Untamed: Reactivating a Missional Form of Discipleship* (Grand Rapids: Baker, 2010), 29.

3. N. T. Wright, *Following Jesus: Biblical Reflections on Discipleship* (Grand Rapids: Eerdmans, 1995), 34.

4. Michael J. Gorman, *Cruciformity: Paul's Narrative Spirituality of the Cross* (Grand Rapids: Eerdmans, 2001), 20.

5. Ibid., 5.

6. Jeffrey P. Greenman, "The Shape of Christian Leadership," 2, http://www.tyndale.ca/leadership/files/.

7. Ibid., 2, 3.

8. W. E. Vine, Merrill F. Unger, and William White Jr., *Vine's Complete Expository Dictionary of Old and New Testament Words* (Nashville: Thomas Nelson, 1985), 138.

9. John MacArthur, "Christ Humbled, Christ Exalted: Jesus' Death Shows Us How to Live," www.BibleBB.com.

10. John Piper, *Brothers: We Are Not Professionals* (Nashville: Mentor, 2003), 194–95.

11. Wright, *Following Jesus*, 40.

12. Lesslie Newbigin, *The Light Has Come: An Exposition of the Fourth Gospel* (Grand Rapids: Eerdmans, 1982), 268.

13. Michael Polanyi, *Personal Knowledge: Toward a Postcritical Philosophy* (Chicago: University of Chicago Press, 1974), 53.

14. Ibid.

15. Quoted by Len Hjalmarson, "Kingdom Leadership in the Postmodern Era," *The Next Reformation*, http://nextreformation.com/wp-admin/resources/Leadership.pdf. This article also appeared in *Reality Magazine* in 2004 and on the Christianity Today Canadian website in 2005. Cited August 2009.

Chapter 5 Breathing Shalom

1. Nancy Jo Sales, "The Suspects Wore Louboutins," *Vanity Fair*, March 2010, 200.

2. Snyder, *Liberating the Church*, 11.

3. Matthew 19:28.

4. Newbigin, *The Light Has Come*, 268.

5. Lucas Conley, *Obsessive Branding Disorder*, quoted in *Adbusters* 83 (May/June 2009).

6. Gustavo Gutiérrez, *We Drink from Our Own Wells: The Spiritual Journey of a People* (New York: Orbis, 2003).

7. Brad Harper and Paul Louis Metzger, *Exploring Ecclesiology: An Evangelical and Ecumenical Introduction* (Grand Rapids: Brazos, 2009), 263–64.

8. http://www.brainyquote.com/quotes/quotes/v/vincentvan106038.html.

9. John Mulvey, "The Twilight World of Bjork," August 11, 2001, quoted in Sheridan Voysey, *Unseen Footprints: Encountering the Divine along the Journey of Life* (Sydney: Scripture Union, 2005), 55.

10. Evelyn Underhill, *Man and the Supernatural*, 170, quoted in Peter Williams, "Aesthetic Arguments for the Existence of God," *Quodlibet Online Journal of Christian Theology and Philosophy* 3, no. 3 (Summer 2001).

11. Anthony O'Hear, *After Progress*, quoted in Voysey, *Unseen Footprints*, 59.

12. David Dale, *Essential Places: A Traveller's Alphabet of Essential Places* (Sydney: Picador, 1996), 24.

13. For more of my views on creation care see my earlier book *Exiles: Living Missionally in a Post-Christian Culture* (Peabody, MA: Hendrickson, 2006), especially chap. 10, "Exiles and the Earth," 229–50.

14. Wright, *Simply Christian*, 236.

15. Ben Katt, an essay written in conjunction with the *Seattle Times*' collaborative project on family homelessness, http://seattletimes.nwsource.com/flatpages/local/invisible families.html.

Chapter 6 Moving into the Neighborhood

1. Kenneth Bailey, *Jesus Through Middle Eastern Eyes* (London: SPCK, 2008) and *Poet and Peasant* and *Through Peasant Eyes: A Literary-Cultural Approach to the Parables in Luke*, combined edition (Grand Rapids: Eerdmans, 1983/2000).

2. Darrell Guder, *The Incarnation and the Church's Witness* (Eugene, OR: Wipf and Stock, 1999), xii–xiii.

3. John M. Perkins, afterword, in Paul Louis Metzger, *Consuming Jesus: Beyond Race and Class Divisions in a Consumer Church* (Eerdmans, Grand Rapids, 2007), 174–75.

4. www.movein.to (cited May 28, 2010).

5. For more information on the Eden network, see http://www.eden-network.org/ Groups/66860/Eden_Network.aspx.

6. Ross Langmead, *The Word Made Flesh: Towards an Incarnational Missiology* (Lanham, MD: University Press of America, 2004), 219.

7. Darrell Guder, *The Missional Church: A Vision for the Sending of the Church in North America* (Grand Rapids: Eerdmans, 1999), 51.

8. Michka Assayas, *Bono on Bono* (London: Hodder and Stoughton, 2005), 125.

9. Kristin Jack, ed., *The Sound of Worlds Colliding: Stories of Radical Discipleship from Servants to Asia's Urban Poor* (Phnom Penh: Hawaii Printing House, 2009), 127.

10. Marilynne Robinson, *Gilead: A Novel* (New York: Picador, 2004), 14.

11. Perkins, cited in Metzger, *Consuming Jesus*, 174–75.

12. Christine Sine, http://godspace.wordpress.com/2010/03/04/where-is-jesus-in-your-neighbourhood/ (cited March 4, 2010).

13. Ibid.

14. "What's Going On at Masa," March 2010 edition. For more on Masa, see http://www.masaofechopark.com.

15. Summarized from Gary Nelson, *Borderland Churches: A Congregation's Introduction to Missional Living* (St. Louis: Chalice Press, 2008), 150–53.

16. Alan Roxburgh, *Reaching a New Generation: Strategies for Tomorrow's Church* (Downers Grove, IL: InterVarsity, 1993), 105.

Conclusion

1. Jack, *Sound of Worlds Colliding*, 121–22.
2. Ibid.
3. Bosch, *Transforming Mission*, 391.
4. Jack, *Sound of Worlds Colliding*, 201.

Michael Frost is an internationally recognized Australian missiologist and one of the leading voices in the missional church movement. His books are required reading in colleges and seminaries around the world, and he is much sought after as an international conference speaker.

Michael is the vice principal of Morling College and the founding director of the Tinsley Institute, a mission study center located at Morling College in Sydney, Australia. He is the author or editor of twelve theological books, including *Jesus the Fool, Seeing God in the Ordinary*, and *Exiles*. He is particularly noted for his collaboration on three books with missiologist Alan Hirsch, the best known being *The Shaping of Things to Come*. These books explore a missional framework for the church in a postmodern era. Their popularity has seen him regularly speaking at conferences in the US, the UK, and across Europe, and as far afield as Nairobi, Rio de Janeiro, and Moscow.

He is the founder of the missional Christian community *smallboatbigsea*, based in Manly in Sydney's north, and the weekly religion columnist for *The Manly Daily*.

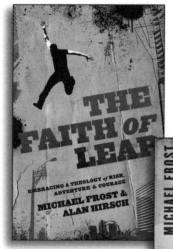
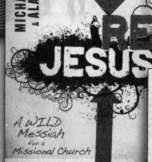

Also from
MICHAEL FROST

Jesus the Fool

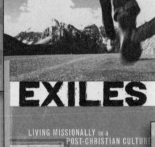

Exiles

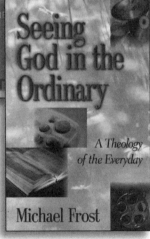

Seeing God in the Ordinary

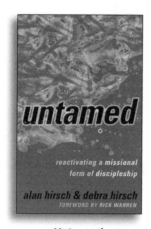
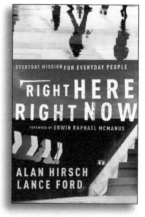
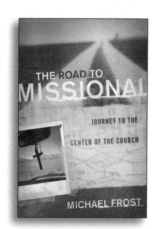

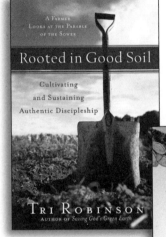

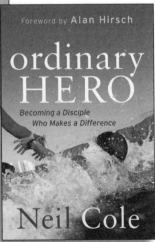